Sexting

Teaching Gender

Volume 3

Series Editor
Patricia Leavy
USA

Scope
Teaching Gender publishes monographs, anthologies and reference books that deal centrally with gender and/or sexuality. The books are intended to be used in undergraduate and graduate classes across the disciplines. The series aims to promote social justice with an emphasis on feminist, multicultural and critical perspectives.

Please email queries to the series editor at pleavy7@aol.com

Sexting

Gender and Teens

Judith Davidson
University of Massachusetts, USA

SENSE PUBLISHERS
ROTTERDAM / BOSTON / TAIPEI

A C.I.P. record for this book is available from the Library of Congress.

ISBN 978-94-6209-849-7 (paperback)
ISBN 978-94-6209-850-3 (hardback)
ISBN 978-94-6209-851-0 (e-book)

Published by: Sense Publishers,
P.O. Box 21858, 3001 AW Rotterdam, The Netherlands
https://www.sensepublishers.com/

Printed on acid-free paper

TABLE OF CONTENTS

ACKNOWLEDGMENTS

My first thanks go to Andrew Harris, professor in the University of Massachusetts Lowell Department of Criminal Justice, who included me in the original study of teens and sexting that led to this work on gender. You have always been generous, insightful, humorous, and kind.

Thanks also to everyone who served on that research team: co-PIs Carl Paternite, Elizabeth Letourneau, and Karin Tusinski-Miofski; thanks also to those who were so helpful in the focus group work: Cricket Meeham, Amy Wilms, and Sarah Hales.

On the UMass Lowell side, we were very lucky to have many wonderful student helpers, including Maryann Ford, Lindsay Tucker, Rob Tanso, Deborah Paul, and Helen Ricci. A very special thanks to Shanna Thompson, who served as research assistant extraordinaire, working with all components of the project.

I also give thanks to the Center for Women and Work at the University of Massachusetts Lowell, from Meg Bond, Director, to all the great associates I have worked with, and students and staff who make CWW such a wonderful place at which to explore the intricacies of gender in today's world. Sarah Kuhn, a special shout out to you for your continued encouragement.

Many UMass Lowell doctoral students have assisted through their work in my qualitative research class; your help was much appreciated.

In the background, encouraging me since my own doctoral school days, Bertram Bruce and Liora Bresler of the University of Illinois; thanks again!

It has been a pleasure to work with Patricia Leavy, Editor of the *Teaching Gender* series at Sense Publishers. Many thanks also to Lori Stone Handelman for her editorial assistance.

Bob, you know you get my thanks too for abiding with the ups and downs of my writing process—and thanks also to our extended families in Colorado and California. Thanks to Sarah (dog), Scooby and Leah (cats), for your affection and patience.

CHAPTER 1

GENDER, YOUTH, AND INTIMACY AS SEEN THROUGH THE LENS OF SEXTING

This is a book about gender, youth, and the search for sexual intimacy, or what I would call the human curriculum of sexuality. It is concerned with the ways adolescents learn how to become sexual beings in today's digital world. In particular, I seek to shed light on the ways society shapes adolescent lives and futures through gendered views, expectations, and social practices.

The data for this topic came from a study examining views of teen sexting from the perspective of teens (girls and boys), caregivers and parents, and other adults—educators, lawmakers, youth workers, etc. (Harris, Davidson, Letourneau, Paternite, & Miofsky, 2013). While sexting, meaning the sharing of sexually explicit messages via digital means, is everywhere in this work, at the same time I can say that sexting is merely instrumental, a means to an end. The end, in this case, is gender and the ways gender is a force in shaping teen lives in today's digital era.

The goal of this work is to take you deep into the perspectives of these four audiences—teen girls, teen boys, caregivers and parents, and other adults who work with and for teens—as they talk about teen sexuality and today's digital world through the lens of sexting. Listening to these parties debate the meaning of sexting, the motivations propelling teens to engage in sexting (or not), and the ways girls and boys are perceived when they engage in such behavior gives us access to a world of information about the ways gender is embedded in the human curriculum of sexuality during the adolescent years.

While this book is not about what to do about sexting—how to promote, restrict, curtail, legislate or discipline it—the study does reveal information about gaps, problems, perceptions and misperceptions in current social and institutional practices that suggest ways to better address the human curriculum of sexuality during adolescence, and to make sense of the way it shapes gender expectations and behavior, and thus, life paths. For this reason, a discussion of the human curriculum of sexuality, as I am calling it, may be a good starting point for this study.

1

THE HUMAN CURRICULUM OF SEXUALITY

The primary focus of this book is gender and the ways youth navigate the human curriculum of sexuality. When I use the term 'human curriculum of sexuality' I am referring to all the ways youth, meaning young people primarily of high school age, have available to them to explore issues of sexuality and make decisions about their own sexual and gendered identity and the directions it will take them. These explorations can come in the form of parental conversations, talks with peers, input from media figures, and formal education. This curriculum is carried out in all aspects of their lives as they learn to understand their sexuality, navigate sexual encounters, and gain experience about the meaning of relationships. It happens in school and out of school, at the mall, in the park, and at parties with friends. It happens at sports events, family outings, and shopping for clothing. Youth are learning and being taught about matters of gender and sexuality through a curriculum that is part personal narrative, part peer social engagement, part adult interaction, and in today's world, part digital culture.

Three critical components of the human curriculum of sexuality are gender, sexuality, and intimate relationships. The first two terms, gender and sexuality, require special clarification. After reviewing definitions from several sources, the Wikipedia descriptions of these terms work best for my discussion as they are specific and yet nuanced compared to many I have read.

> **Gender** is the range of physical, biological, mental and behavioral characteristics pertaining to, and differentiating between, masculinity and femininity. Depending on the context, the term may refer to biological sex (i.e., the state of being male, female or intersex), sex-based social structures (including gender roles and other social roles), or gender identity ("Gender," n.d.).

> **Human sexuality** is the capacity to have erotic experiences and responses. A person's sexual orientation may influence their sexual interest and attraction for another person. Sexuality can have biological, physical, emotional, or spiritual aspects. The biological and physical aspects of sexuality largely concern the reproductive functions of the sexes (including the human sexual response cycle), and the basic biological drive that exists in all species. Physical, as well as emotional, aspects of sexuality also include the bond that exists between individuals, and is expressed through profound feelings or physical manifestations of emotions of love, trust, and caring.

Spiritual aspects of sexuality concern an individual's spiritual connection with others. Sexuality additionally impacts and is impacted by cultural, political, legal, and philosophical aspects of life. It can refer to issues of morality, ethics and theology, or religion ("Human Sexuality," n.d.).

As young people approach these three areas in their lives, the following questions emerge for them:

– Gender
  What kind of gendered person am I? How do I fit myself within gendered structures? What opportunities or challenges will my gendered identity contain? How will I perform my gender? Will my gender work for me or against me?
– Sexuality
  How is sexuality part of my gendered being? How do I express my sexuality? What's appropriate where and when? Whose advice should I listen to about the issues of sexuality?
– Relationships
  How can I be intimate with someone? How do you start getting close to someone? How do you flirt? When do you know if it is safe to trust? What should I believe? What is sex all about? Should I have sex with this person or that?

With the advent of the Internet and other digital media, youth explorations of gender, sexuality, and intimate relationships have necessarily included technology and the recent phenomenon called sexting.

DIGITAL TECHNOLOGIES + SEX = SEXTING

Sexting is a phenomenon of our new digital technologies. It is a term coined to explain the ways human beings have found to use these new tools to explore and express sexuality.

As with the terms gender and human sexuality, I am also using the definition of sexting provided by Wikipedia:

Sexting is the act of sending sexually explicit messages, primarily between mobile phones. The term was first popularized in the early 21st century, and is a portmanteau of sex and texting, where the latter is meant in the wide sense of sending a text possibly with images. In August 2012, the word sexting was listed for the first time in Merriam-Webster's Collegiate Dictionary ("Sexting," n.d.).

Sexting seems to be everywhere. Celebrities such as Tiger Woods, Miley Cyrus, and Rihanna do it (Weintrub, 2011); politicians do it—witness the case of New York politician Anthony Weiner—and, to our horror, young people do it (Brunker, 2009). Where did it come from? Where is it leading us? Is it evil? Is it another form of intimacy? Is it a result of being digital? Is it the first step down a path of depravity from which one will never return?

Public imagination is captured by the ease with which casual photos can be broadcast across the world. Is this why we feel digital media is so much more lethal than an old-fashioned romantic phone call, a posted love letter, or a Playboy pin-up?

Sexting came to the fore at a time when many said our society had become noticeably more open sexually. Where should we draw the line in regard to what can be shown? What is proper attire? As Myspace emerged—only to be surpassed by Facebook, Twitter, YouTube, Vimeo, Instagram, and other digital social media tools—it became increasingly apparent that society was gravitating toward a new relationship to privacy and exposure (boyd, 2014). Adults as well as teens struggle to know what should be shared and what should not (Holson, 2012).

Those who grew up in pre-digital or early digital times (often referred to as digital immigrants) wonder if younger people, whose lives have always been fully immersed in digital culture (referred to as digital natives), would learn to read, write, and think properly in a world like this (Prensky, 2001). They could see the opportunities technology had opened up for young people in so many fields, from science to computing, graphic novels to gaming; however, they were also scared of the dangers young people faced in the wild and wholly digital landscape. Would the developmental imperatives of adolescence—to become gendered, sexual beings with the capacity for rich and meaningful intimacy with significant others—be derailed by social media and its dangers and, in particular, sexting?

THE STUDY BEHIND THIS STUDY:
OR WHERE THE DATA CAME FROM

These issues surrounding sexting led to the study undergirding this book (Harris et al., 2013). Led by Andrew Harris, faculty member in the Criminal Justice Department of the University of Massachusetts Lowell, the study asked high school-age teens, caregivers, and other educators and youth workers about their views of teen sexting. The study was conducted by research teams in three states: Massachusetts, Ohio, and South Carolina.

I was a member of the lead Massachusetts research team in charge of overall organization of the qualitative research component of the study.

As this study got underway, sexting had just begun to become a significant concern within educational and law enforcement circles. Initial research into the topic had been primarily in the form of surveys (Cox Communications and National Center for Missing and Exploited Children, 2009; Lenhart, 2009; Lenhart, Ling, Campbell, & Purcell, 2010; National Campaign to Prevent Teen and Unplanned Pregnancy, 2008). These first surveys focused on young people as the subjects with the aim of learning who was sexting, how much sexting was going on, under what circumstances it occurred, and how dangerous it might be. During the course of our study, surveys continued to be released providing more refined perspectives on the issue of sexting (Lenhart et al., 2011; Madden, Lenhart, Duggan, Cortesi, & Gasser, 2013; Mitchell, Wolak, & Finkelhor, 2007; Mitchell, Finkelhor, Jones, & Wolak, 2012; Strassberg, McKinnon, Sustaita, & Rullo, 2012; Temple et al., 2012). In those first years, researchers scrambled to identify literature related to the topic (e.g. Ford, Tucker, Thompson, Davidson & Harris, 2012; Marwick, Murgia-Diaz, & Palfrey, 2010).

However, at the time this study was initiated there was virtually no work that looked at the issue of sexting from the emic, or deeply insider, perspectives of young people; that is, how did they conceptualize the very meaning of the term sexting? What were the practices they identified as belonging with this term? What were the motivations, values, and concerns young people associated with sexting? Finally, what did they understand of the personal or legal dangers related to these practices? What did they think were the best ways to help young people understand and avoid dangerous behaviors in this realm? And finally, the issue of concern in this volume, how does gender affect the views and the challenges young people face in regard to the issues sexting raises for them?

We also lacked information about the ways adolescents' significant others—caregivers, educators, youth workers and law enforcement—understood the phenomenon of sexting or knew how to address it within their organizations. An important exception was the work of David Finkelhor and his colleagues at the University of New Hampshire's Crimes Against Children Research Center, who examined the ways sexting was coming to the attention of law enforcement (Wolak, Finkelhor, & Mitchell, 2012). Harris and colleagues provide a comprehensive table of the survey research produced as researchers turned their sights to studying this phenomenon ("Appendix 1," 2013).

Not surprisingly, the policies for dealing with teen sexting within schools and among legal forces were a hodgepodge of under-reaction, over-reaction, and everything in between. As with teens, it wasn't really clear how adults who were important to teens were conceptualizing the notion of sexting, nor how their beliefs and understandings converged or diverged in regard to the best ways with which to address the phenomenon (Bazelon, 2013; Palfrey, 2008).

Lacking access to other voices and sources of information, it is not surprising that many adults assumed sexting was an extremely dangerous act practiced by the most deviant types, even though we lacked knowledge of whether this was the case or not. Indeed, as we learned in conducting our own research, many people—young and old—are still unsure of what the term means, let alone the practices it encompasses.

The *sexting study*, as I will refer to the Harris et al (2013) work, sought to contribute knowledge that would fill in two important areas of society's understanding of sexting: 1) youth perspectives on sexting, and 2) the views of adults engaged with youth (in and beyond the home) regarding youth and sexting. To obtain this kind of information, we elected to use a mixture of tools: surveys to provide background information on participant demographics and to lay a comparable foundation of information on digital practices within and across our groups, and structured focus group interviews to provide richer data on practice, process, and belief regarding the topic than what had been possible in earlier surveys. Data were gathered from participants in three states—Massachusetts, Ohio, and South Carolina—representing contrasting regions of the United States: the Northeast, Midwest, and South. A total of 123 teens, 92 parents or caregivers, and 117 others in teens' lives were interviewed. (For more details on the sample and methodology see Chapter 2.)

THE GENESIS AND DEVELOPMENT OF THIS BOOK

This book represents the coming together of diverse strands of my own background as a scholar at a particular time and place in my academic life. These strands include a focus on gender, an understanding of adolescence, and the place of new digital technologies in our lives.

Why Gender?

With a topic like sexting, it would be impossible to ignore outright the topic of gender, but it would be fair to say that when I started work on the initial study, gender was only one of many things on my radar. In designing the original research study, we assumed gender was important, but we wanted to come to the issues with an open mind, to discover whatever new ideas the research process might reveal. The interview questions asked youth and adults to reflect on the ways they perceived sexting to be related to gender expectations. Moreover, we arranged to interview male and female youth in separate groups in order to allow them to speak about gendered issues without pressure.

As I read and re-read the interview transcripts in all four pods of collected data, the pervasiveness of gendered perspectives could not be denied. For instance, I realized that even discussions about which technologies youth used (boys were playing more video games) or television shows they watched (girls were watching more daytime interview shows) ended up having significant gender implications. This was also true for adults, in different ways. For instance, mothers supervised issues related to youth behavior (including technology) in different ways than did fathers. Gender could not be ignored or dismissed.

Two sets of doctoral students read and analyzed portions of the adult data as part of an assignment for the qualitative research methods course I teach. The Fall 2012 class reviewed 'other adult' data, and the Fall 2013 class reviewed parent/caregiver data. Both groups were struck by the pervasiveness of gendered expectations in the comments made by adults. In particular, they were surprised to read how often girls were blamed in regard to sexting incidents, while boys were often seen as hapless victims. The interpretations drawn by these two classes were harbingers of what I was to learn about gender from the data as I engaged in the subsequent analysis for this book.

During the same time I was serving on the research team for this project, I was participating as a faculty associate at the Center for Women and Work on our campus, an interdisciplinary group of scholars dedicated to a better understanding of gender issues. I presented the findings of the sexting study and they were quick to notice and point out issues related to gender that were embedded in the data, offering good resources and probing questions.

Interactions with scholars outside our campus also led to more questions about the ways gender was figuring in this data about sexting. Feminist scholar Jessica Ringrose from the University of London's Institute of Education visited our campus to discuss the qualitative research work she had recently undertaken on sexting and teens in the UK (Ringrose, Gill, Livingstone, & Harvey, 2012). Her visit provided another opportunity to consider how gender was at work within the data we were reviewing. Her study also flagged gender issues, and in particular mentioned that "girls [were] most adversely affected" (2012, p.7).

Presentations at conferences and published papers provided more opportunities to talk about the gendered issues emerging from the sexting study (Davidson, 2014a; Davidson, 2014c; Davidson, Harris, Thompson, Tucker, & Ford, 2012; Davidson, Thompson, & Harris, 2014).

As a result of these investigations I can now report that I approach this work with an orientation toward gender that is concerned about issues of performance (Butler, 2008), orientation (Ahmed, 2006), and restrictions or disciplining (Foucault, 1975/1977; Griffin, 2011). Gender, as I construe it, is always discursively and culturally constituted. Thus, it exists within the constraints of historical understanding and political regimes of power. By historical understanding, I refer to the prior practices by which we divide and treat those identified as male versus those identified as female (as well as other gender designations). Likewise, in regard to gender and power, I consider the ways these perceived differences are organized to support or oppress individuals and groups based upon their gendered affiliation.

As a qualitative researcher, I bear in mind the concerns regarding gender that have emerged through methodological discussions, where silencing is both a matter of study (gendered silences in a society) as well as an issue of methodological approach (the gendered blinders that a researcher might be wearing) (Hesse-Biber, 2012).

Adolescence and Technology

Unlike my approach to gender—from emergent to focused—I came to my notion of adolescence and technology with more fully fleshed-out principles. In an earlier time in my life I was a staff member at the Center for Early Adolescence at the University of North Carolina, heading up the Project on Adolescent Literacy (Davidson & Koppenhaver, 1993). That experience did much to shape my philosophy of adolescence as a healthy period of development in the lifespan, teaching me that youth are not inherently unbalanced, no more so than at any other particular period of our lives.

Our sexting project team was well staffed with psychologists possessing deep knowledge of research on adolescents, including Cricket Meehan and Carl Paternite of Miami University in Ohio, and Elizabeth Letourneau, now at John Hopkins University. They were all advocates of a positive philosophy of adolescence that had strong resonance with mine. So too Harris, with his background in criminal justice, brought a perspective on prevention that was complementary to a positive view of adolescence.

Karin Tusinski-Miofsky, a criminal justice colleague of Harris's with expertise in issues of teens and bullying, also brought a positive focus on youth and their capacities.

In addition to my earlier work on adolescence, I also had deep roots in the arena of technology and social practice. As a graduate student working in the field of literacy, I was drawn to perspectives of reading as a technology embedded in specific socio-cultural and historical practices (Davidson, 2014b). As a post-graduate, my first job was as research director for a study of Internet implementation in a suite of four schools (K-12) on the Hanau American Army Base in Hanau, Germany (Davidson, 2004; Davidson & Olson, 2003). When I morphed into a college professor at the University of Massachusetts Lowell, I found myself immersed in exploring the ways qualitative research technology not only worked, but how it was situated as a social and cultural practice within the field of qualitative research and where the technological future of this field lay, and why (Cisneros & Davidson, 2012; Davidson & diGregorio 2011a; 2011b; diGregorio & Davidson, 2008). Based upon my experience studying technology in K-12 settings, for many years I have taught an online class in the University of Massachusetts Lowell Graduate School of Education called "Planning Technology and School Improvement," where I undertake ethnographic explorations in school technology practices with a wide variety of students from diverse geographical locations. Each of the experiences mentioned above sharpened my technology chops by providing me opportunities to think critically about technology from philosophical, methodological, and experiential perspectives. Little did I know, but I was being readied for sexting—a phenomenon that was just on the horizon.

As a group, our sexting research team felt a strong connection to the view of adolescence in a digital society presented by Ito and her colleagues in the three-year ethnographic study titled "Kids' Informal Learning with Digital Media Project," funded by the John D. and Catherine T. MacArthur Foundation (Ito, 2010). This study laid out a perspective on youth development and a notion of media ecology that was particularly instructive for the work our team was about to undertake. Out of that research study have come a number of studies that continue to define the digital landscape in which youth now live (e.g., boyd, 2014; Lange, 2014; Watkins, 2009). The Connected Learning initiative of Mimi Ito, a leader on the earlier MacArthur study, continues to expand the insights of that ethnographic work into practical experiments with digital learning and youth (connectedlearning.tv, 2014). This body of work examining youth and digital experiences seeks to understand youth practices and perspectives in regard to the use of new digital technologies. It does not presume guilt or innocence; rather, it examines the ways technology is used, the value it accrues and provides to youth, and the possibilities it offers for learning, both in formal and informal contexts.

Taken as a whole—my experiences researching adolescence and educational technologies, the research regarding adolescence and technology that has played an important role in the design of the original sexting study, and this subsequent work on gender—I can state that first, last, and forever I believe adolescence to be a normal stage of human development no more peculiar or deviant than infancy or old age. However, by virtue of physical development and cultural expectations, teens face unique social, emotional, and intellectual challenges. Today's teens, growing up as they are in a world of digital technologies, are not better or worse off than teens of past generations; rather, as dana boyd describes, "… what teens are doing as they engage in networked publics makes sense. At the same time, coming to terms with life in a networked era is not necessarily easy or obvious. Rather, it's complicated" (2014, p. 28).

THE MEDIA

By media, I refer to the vast, surrounding bubble of informational, recreational, and persuasive materials—commercial and non-commercial—that are disseminated in a vast number of forms, from ad flyers and television shows to web pages and fashion magazines. We swim in the midst of these messaging forms, their words and pronouncements, symbols and images.

Our notions of media are embedded in the temporal experience of our lives. Thus, we experience the flow of media as past and present, as this Massachusetts mother illustrates: "And even as you watch media, and TV, and movies …, things that were unacceptable to be shown or said on TV today, are just there. I mean, 20 years ago, you'd never see a Victoria's Secret model on daytime TV. That would be on a blocked channel, but now it's OK."

The media is deeply implicated in discussions about sexting. It reports on incidents, comments on the meaning of these incidents, and speculates about how to address these concerns. Media attention to sexting occurs in the news and on talk shows, shows up as the story line in movies and various television series, and has even been the subject of commercials (the commercial for cell phones with the old lady shooting a photo under her dress). It would be fair to say that media attention to the sexting issue was a primary impetus for the original sexting study.

As the sexting study team read through the transcripts, we were struck by the ways this nebulous thing known as 'the media' rose to the fore. Teens, parents and caregivers, and other adults had all been exposed to the idea of sexting from the media, and there were many specific references to where and when they heard about sexting on TV, a music video, or another source. These references were likely to be raised when we asked, "Where did you first hear about sexting?"

Flying further under the radar, that is, not identifiable by specific events, were the generalized discussions about the media's presentation of sexuality and gender. These references emerged in diverse sections of the text, but particularly as youth and adults considered the motivations for sexting. It also arose as youth considered adult perspectives and vice versa.

In this text, media will be a significant consideration as I explore notions of sexuality and gender as revealed through the lens of sexting.

CONCLUSIONS

From this point on you will be entering the world of teens, their caregivers, and others who care about this age group. While I have drawn conclusions and made choices about the data presented, as much as possible I have allowed their voices to speak. As a reader, I want you to hear youth and adults describing their world views, and as facilitator of this discussion, I will try to stay in the background.

Following this introduction is a brief chapter describing the characteristics of the participants in the study and more background on the methodology of the study. The volume is then arranged so each of the four communities of speakers—girls, boys, parents/caregivers, and other adults—are heard speaking from their own unique positions. Each is given its own chapter in which to hold forth on their views. The first section, youth voices, includes the chapter on girls and then one on boys, followed by a comparison of the youth perspectives. Likewise, the second section, adult voices, starts with a chapter about parental and caregiver perspectives followed by a chapter that describes the views of what I will call other adults, and this, too, is followed by a brief comparison of the two adult chapters.

The final chapter of the book draws back from the intimate world of the participants in the sexting study to the wider world of the findings and their implications. In other words, what conclusions can we draw from these conversations? What indication do they give us of what young people are learning about gender, and why? How do these conversations help us to better understand the human curriculum of sexuality, the role of gender within it, and the ways adults are, or are not, playing a useful role as instructors in this field?

CHAPTER 2

PEOPLE, PLACES, AND PROCESSES

This chapter introduces you to the people, places, and processes that led to this book. As described in the first chapter, the data used for this book were derived from a project on teens and sexting (Harris et al., 2013), which I refer to as the sexting study. The processes described here span the research processes of the initial study, as well as reference the subsequent research processes that were applied in this secondary study.

PEOPLE AND PLACES

The people comprised two large groups—youth and adults—that can be further subdivided into two smaller groups each. The youth group was made up of a female and a male subgroup. The adult group comprised parents and caregivers and then a group of what I term 'other adults: ' individuals who work with and for adolescents.

The four groups of participants were drawn from the Northeast (Massachusetts), the Midwest (Ohio), and the South (South Carolina). At each of the three locations, a research team conducted interviews with the two youth groups (males and females separately), followed in the second stage by interviews with caretakers or parents, and finally by focus group interviews with individuals in the 'other adults' group.

Pseudonyms for the place locations within each state are: Massachusetts: Romney, Andrews, and Gateway City; Ohio: Native, Norse, and Astro; and South Carolina: Wes, Brad, and Norton; and a fourth Make-Up group.

Research design and the informed consent process were carefully reviewed prior to undertaking on-site work. In this secondary study, I conformed to the ethical guidelines outlined in the first study. To maintain confidentiality, all participants were initially assigned a number designation in the focus group, which was used for the transcription. The number designation was later changed to a pseudonym for ease of reading.

At each site, we administered an anonymous survey before the focus group interview to collect demographic and technology-use data. In the case of youth, after the focus group interview we also conducted a second anonymous survey in which we asked questions about sexting practices.

CHAPTER 2

Youth

There were 123 youth who participated in this study, with slightly more female than male participants. Youth were interviewed in 18 different focus groups, separated by gender—three female and three male focus groups each in Massachusetts and Ohio, and four female and four male groups in South Carolina, where lower attendance required a male and female make-up group. Our aim was to focus on three high school communities in each state. We achieved this goal in Ohio and South Carolina. In Massachusetts we worked with two high school communities and, to recruit our third group, one non-profit organization with close ties to a high school.

All youth were attending high school and had a median age of 17, meaning that the majority were in their junior and senior years. Looking across the participants, they not only represented a range of regions, but the students themselves attended schools that were urban and non-urban. Racially, nearly half were white (46.3%), almost a third were African-American (30.1%), and the rest was represented by other racial or cultural groups. The exception to this pattern was South Carolina, where white students were the minority (10.3%) and 79.3% were African-American students.

Although not presented in Table 1, my own review of the youth demographics shows our participants came from diverse family formations—mother and father, parent and step-parent, single mother or less frequently single father, and in some instances another form of caretaker.

Parents

Parent focus groups were recruited from the same high school communities from which we drew our youth participants. Parents were recruited several months subsequent to conducting the youth component of the study and may or may not have been parents of participants in the youth focus group.

Women far outnumbered men in the sample (82.6% women to 17.4% men). While the median income was $80-90,000, this figure is inflated by higher salaries in Massachusetts and Ohio; participants in South Carolina had significantly lower salaries.

A higher majority of parent participants were white, and again the greater number of African-American participants were located in South Carolina.

Table 1. Characteristics of Youth Sample*

	TOTAL	*MA*	*OH*	*SC*
N	123	42	52	29
Gender				
Male	44.7%	45.2%	44.2%	44.8%
Female	55.3%	54.8%	55.8%	55.2%
Median Age	17	17	17	18
Grade Level				
9th	13.0%	9.5%	15.4%	13.8%
10th	19.5%	23.8%	17.3%	17.2%
11th	34.1%	31.0%	42.3%	24.1%
12th	32.5%	35.7%	25.0%	41.4%
Race/Ethnicity				
White	46.3%	50.0%	63.5%	10.3%
Black/African	30.1%	9.5%	19.2%	79.3%
Hispanic/Latino	4.9%	11.9%	1.9%	0.0%
Asian/Pacific	9.8%	14.3%	11.5%	0.0%
Other	8.1%	14.3%	3.8%	6.9%

Table 2. Characteristics of Parent Sample*

	Total	*MA*	*OH*	*SC*
N	92	20	46	26
Gender				
Male	17.4%	25.0%	19.6%	7.7%
Female	82.6%	75.0%	80.4%	92.3%
Median Income	$80K-$90K	$90K-$100K	$100K-$150K	< $10K
Race/Ethnicity				
White	62.0%	80.0%	71.7%	30.8%
Black/African	31.5%	15.0%	21.7%	61.5%
Hispanic/Latino	3.3%	0.0%	4.3%	3.8%
Asian/Pacific	1.1%	0.0%	2.2%	0.0%
Other	2.2%	5.0%	0.0%	3.8%

Other Adults

Unlike the youth and parent or caregiver groups, our 'other adults' groups included, but were not limited to, the three high school community areas in each state. We were quite opportunistic in seeking out these adults, overlapping with conferences, double booking with school professional development days, and any other legitimate ways we could garner participation from these very hard-working individuals. As a result, the participant numbers and groupings varied. The 53 participants in Massachusetts were members of six focus groups conducted in a single morning at a local conference. There were three focus groups in Ohio (33 participants), and three in South Carolina (31 participants).

Table 3. Characteristics of Other Adults Sample*

	Total	MA	OH	SC
N	117	53	33	31
Gender				
Male	23.1%	28.3%	21.2%	16.1%
Female	76.9%	71.7%	78.8%	83.9%
Race/Ethnicity				
White	74.4%	88.7%	57.6%	67.7%
Black/African American	20.5%	5.7%	39.4%	25.8%
Hispanic/Latino	2.6%	3.8%	0.0%	3.2%
Asian/Pacific Islander	0.9%	1.9%	0.0%	0.0%
Other	0.9%	0.0%	0.0%	3.2%
Role				
Classroom Teacher	20.5%	13.2%	3.0%	51.6%
Health/Wellness Educator	9.4%	13.2%	9.1%	3.2%
Guidance Counselor	15.4%	22.6%	9.1%	9.7%
Law Enforcement	13.7%	18.9%	18.2%	0.0%
Other	41.0%	32.1%	60.6%	35.5%
Years of Experience				
Median	11	13	12	9
Less than 1	2.6%	3.8%	3.0%	0.0%
1 to 10	46.2%	41.5%	39.4%	61.3%
11 to 20	29.1%	34.0%	33.3%	16.1%
21 and above	18.8%	17.0%	18.2%	22.6%

In the 'other adults' groups, as with the parent groups, women dominated (76.9% compared to 23.1% of men). Adult participant focus group members were also primarily white (74%). Interestingly, the largest number of African-American adult members were in Ohio (39.4% compared to 5.7% in Massachusetts and 25.8% in South Carolina).

Those in the 'other adults' groups self-reported on their role, providing us with multiple titles for the same or only slightly different jobs. In developing the final report we consolidated these into a limited number of categories. As illustrated in the table, classroom teachers predominated in the South Carolina groups (not surprisingly because those groups were held at the schools), whereas a broader representation of different roles occurred in Massachusetts (where focus groups were held at a professional development event on the topic of sexting).

Experience on the job was about evenly divided between those with fewer than 10 years and those with 10 or more years. However, in South Carolina there were a significant number in the youngest and oldest categories, with the smallest number in the 11 to 20 years of experience group.

PROCESSES

The data collected and the processes employed for the initial study were primarily qualitative in nature. This means that depth of research materials and analysis took precedence over breadth or large sample size—although, for a qualitative research interview study we were definitely data-heavy.

There are those who would also ask, "Yes, but what kind of qualitative research were you doing? Is this Grounded Theory? Narrative analysis? Phenomenology? Ethnography? Case study?" In this study I took various kinds of qualitative research approaches into consideration as I tried to find the best path for the work. I will admit to the prejudice I have for an ethnographic approach, definitely leaning toward narrative analysis, and a fondness for the later versions of grounded theory. In this study, rather than subscribe to one brand like applying a statistical formula, I preferred to think of these variations as part of a large swelling river with tributaries, windings, oxbows, and re-connections. In short, the best way to describe the methodological approach is with the broadest term: qualitative research.

Because our research orientation was toward qualitative approaches, in the focus groups participants were asked open-ended questions and encouraged to reflect through narrative. The analysis of this kind of data is a words-to-words approach, rather than a statistical one. This is not to say that quantification is not at work, even in a qualitative research study. Such terms as more, some, a lot, less, are employed in talking about qualitative data, but they are used as synthesizing statements about the narrative whole.

The focus group interview questions covered the same range of topics for all groups, with small variations depending on the role of the participant. All focus group interviews were divided into two components: 1) an opening set of questions about technology use, and 2) a core set of questions related to sexting.

Technology questions provided a safe beginning point for discussion of what could be a difficult topic: the digital side of sex, or sexting. The initial questions in our protocol sought to uncover information about the role of technology in participants' lives, with an emphasis on what they could tell us about technology in teen lives.

In the subsequent portions of the focus group interviews, we sought information from participants on: 1) the way they defined sexting, 2) how they understood its motivations and characteristics—where, why, and with whom they imagined it took place, 3) how teens were communicating to adults and other teens about the topic, 4) what the different parties imagined the consequences to be, and finally 5) participants' suggestions for addressing the issue of sexting.

The analysis process used in the sexting study is amply described in the final report to the United States Department of Juvenile Justice (Harris et al., 2013). That analysis process was conducted with the aid of NVivo software, a tool for storing and organizing qualitative data. At the end of that study I was in possession of a digital database with all the focus group and survey materials coded around the topical areas of the original focus group questions and containing all subsequent emergent coding.

This secondary study, however, aimed to place gender in the primary position and sexting in the ancillary position. This meant conducting another analysis of the materials to review the sexting materials from this new perspective. This also meant I had to forget much of what I thought I knew about the transcribed words, coming to them now with a new outlook.

In reviewing the materials, I wanted to amply describe each of the four views clearly and distinctly, representing their similarities, but also the important differences among them. In conducting my review, I put the youth first, grounding myself in their views before I shifted to the adults.

I also made use of the database as a teaching tool in my doctoral level qualitative research classes, killing two birds with one stone. First, it had always been my dream to have a complex qualitative research database organized in NVivo to use for class assignments. I also wanted my students to use such a database to contribute something to a real research project, rather than just an exercise to demonstrate their skills with the technology. With the database from the sexting study I could do both.

Working individually and in small groups, my Fall 2012 qualitative research class examined the 'other adult' portion of the data, developing working papers on emergent themes. My Fall 2013 class examined the parent/caregiver portion of the data, also developing working papers on emergent themes. The Fall 2012 class was composed of doctoral students from the UMass Lowell Graduate School of Education, while the Fall 2013 class was composed of educational doctoral students as well as several students from other doctoral programs on campus.

Students in the two classes were asked to code and analyze broadly, seeking emergent themes. I explained I had an interest in gender, but did not say much more. They were not asked to code or seek out gender issues. To my surprise, however, in both years gender was the theme that jumped out front and center to my students. The two groups were surprised at the ways parents and fellow educators held different gendered expectations for boys and girls. In particular, they were surprised by the ways girls were held responsible and shamed for sexual acts, and boys were not. Their strong reactions in regard to gender in the data told me there was something important to follow here.

A sabbatical spring semester in 2014 provided the time I needed for a full review of all four components of the data and time to write. In conducting my re-evaluation for this secondary study, I focused primarily on focus group responses related to the questions of what is sexting, what motivates it, and what are the contexts in which it appears.

NOTES TO THE READER

There are a couple of definitions or explanations needed before you dive into the words of the participants.

First, I have made it my convention to describe the youth as girls and boys, rather than young women and young men. This felt the most natural for me. If they had been college age, I think I would have used young women and young men, but girls and boys seemed to keep them in the realm of young people who were still closely connected to the family unit. This is a personal preference.

Second, you will find that I use parents and caregivers interchangeably throughout the text. Again, this is a personal preference. Most in this category were parents, but not all. All who participated in these particular focus groups were playing a significant parenting role to a young person, whether it was an older sibling or grandparent.

Third, going forward I will capitalize the term Other Adults to refer to the focus groups of educators, police officers, counselors, etc. When you encounter the term capitalized, you will know it refers to the focus group category.

Fourth, because this is a double-tiered study, when I speak of the researchers as 'we,' I am referring to the primary study, also referred to as the sexting study (Harris et al., 2013). When I speak in the first person singular, I am referring to this secondary study you are reading now.

Fifth, as you read the following sections, please note that quotations from youth and parent/caregiver groups are referenced by state first, followed by location within the state as designated by a pseudonym. Thus, "Massachusetts: Andrew" refers to a participant from the community of Andrews in Massachusetts. Those in the Other Adult chapter are referenced by state and a focus group designation.

In the following two sections (Section I: Youth, and Section II: Adults), it is my goal to give you a close-up, intense look at the ways each of the four focus groups provided insights on perspectives about gender. When you read a specific chapter you will be reading from that single viewpoint.

There is one significant exception to this rule and that comes in the chapter about boys where I discuss something known as 'the flip.' Here I discuss perspectives from both boys and girls. This was an exception I felt was necessary for a more coherent telling of the story.

For similar reasons, in the two sections where I focus on the viewpoints of the four participant groups, I have resisted the temptation to bring in outside experts to comment on the discussion so you can hear the voices of the participants as clearly as possible. I reserve the experts and their commentary, definitions, or perspectives for the beginning and ending of the book. The heart of the book lies, as I feel it should in a qualitative research study, with the participants.

NOTE

*Data on sample characteristics are quoted from the original study (Harris et al., 2013, pp. 22-23).

SECTION I

INTRODUCTION

YOUTH VOICES

Youth are at the heart of this work. Views from and about youth were the focus of the data from which this story is told. Thus, it is appropriate to begin with the voices of youth.

In this section, you will first hear the perspectives of teen girls (Chapter 3). I will let them describe their understanding of sexting and what sense they make of gender as they navigate this new phenomenon in our society.

In Chapter 4, you will have the opportunity to hear from teen boys. They too will be allowed to speak without interference from girls, parents or other adult experts.

The conclusion of Section I provides space to think comparatively across the girls' and boys' voices before shifting perspectives to the views of adults.

TEEN GIRLS AND THE PHENOMENON OF SEXTING

HOW GIRLS DEFINE SEXTING

Amanda: Sexting—I don't—it's kind of vague to me, because, you know, I've heard a lot about it on TV and news and stuff. It kind of went through a trend for a while, like everything—everybody was talking about all of these charges and stuff coming up, and I guess I don't really have a definition. I don't really know. Inappropriate things being texted or sent via text message?

Interviewer: OK. Like what type of things?

Amanda: Body parts. Inappropriate language—sexual language.

Interviewer: OK. All right. So that's like some of the specific actions, and stuff like that. It sounds like that comes to mind when you hear the term 'sexting.' What about you, Brandi?

Brandi: I agree with Amanda. I mean, I don't really have a basic definition, to summarize the whole sexting thing, but I hear a lot about it. (South Carolina: Wes.)

This quotation from a discussion with girls in South Carolina presents the basic confusion young people expressed when they tried to define sexting. The passage illustrates the variety of associations that clustered together as participants began to think about the topic, ranging from news coverage to technology and connections to sexuality.

In definitional discussions about sexting, there were probably as many questions as there were statements, and much of this questioning related to the relationship of technologies to sexting. Is sexting a text or a photo? Can it be a video? Does it refer to the sending, receiving, forwarding, or accepting? Cell phones are definitely involved, but what about the Internet? Below, three young women from Massachusetts illustrate the complexities young people raised as they thought through the issues of technology and its relationship to the act of sexting.

Haley: I'll admit that I did a 4-5 page research paper on this so I think I might know but before that I'll admit I thought it was sending

> naked pictures. I thought that's what sexting was. But now I
> believe it's sending, receiving or viewing of any sexually explicit
> text or images via a—
>
> Interviewer: A mobile device?
>
> Haley: A media device or anything like that. That's what I wrote in
> my paper and I got an A. (laughter)
>
> Interviewer: So you're saying that it could be on not only cell phones
> but also on like computers and—
>
> Haley: Whatever else people have ... Skype videos, yeah.
>
> Gabrielle: I feel like sexting is a very general term and it's almost
> directed toward texting but there are so many other ways that you
> can be sexual with people not just texting them. Like you can
> have phone sex or you can send pictures emailing or you can
> even like webcam with other people, so.
>
> Becky: I think it's just transformed over time. Because it used to be
> like dirty letters and then it just turned into pictures. Because
> when we were younger it was pictures because no one texted or
> had Skype or anything. But now every more technology, that's
> kind of like the downfall of technology because now you are so
> accessible to everyone that you can do whatever you want with
> technology and people are using it to do whatever they want.
> (Massachusetts: Andrew)

From our discussions with girls about the definition of sexting, we learned
that they generally considered sexting to be a fairly common practice
among teens, although participation may vary widely from individual to
individual. Girls viewed sexting as something that happens across the
lifespan. They indicated that sexting can be regarded as nasty or reasonable,
depending upon the context. Overall, girls were reluctant to define sexting
narrowly as a particular form of technology or a specific form of sexuality.
They were also reluctant to define it too rigidly in terms of relationships,
morality, or danger. Indeed, sexting, like sex and intimacy, was a fluid
concern in girls' minds.

GIRLS' UNDERSTANDING OF THE MOTIVATIONS FOR SEXTING

In analyzing girls' identified motivations for sexting, three areas rose to the
fore as central to girls' understanding of why girls or boys engage in
sexting. The first area was the realm of relationships, and in particular,
romantic relationships, that is, relationships in which girls describe the role
of sexting in the facilitation of creating a specific intimate relationship with
(in the case of our sample) a member of the opposite sex. The second area

was that of peers, social status, and power. This is a vast terrain that takes in many kinds of social relationships as they are enacted in home, school, and community settings. The third area was sexuality—the primal call of the species to engage in intimate sexual acts with another of the same species. These three areas did not represent the sum total of the discussion of motivators, but they were the areas that garnered the greatest attention in conversation with girls. Discussion of sexual predators and seduction by those outside one's social group did not receive much attention from our girl participants. However, I have included the topic here because of the outsized attention it receives from the media.

In discussion of motivations for sexting, girls described girls as most concerned about romantic relationships, although they were well aware girls are also engaged in the exercise of power within social contexts with peers. Girls do not ignore the call of sexuality, but it received relatively less attention in their discussion than these first two areas.

However, when girls spoke of boys' motivations, the picture changed. Girls described boys as inherently competitive, and thus highly motivated to engage in sexting for reasons related to peers, social contexts, and power. Girls perceived boys to have much less capacity for and interest in the kinds of romantic relationships girls seek. Girls also saw boys as highly motivated by the desire to have sex, making this a powerful reason for them to engage in sexting.

Girls offered strong perspectives on what I have come to call beliefs about gender inherency, that is, girls are *this* and boys are *that*. In the focus groups girls tended to portray themselves as more private, seeking to avoid gossip, and yet highly dependent on male opinion. At the same time, some girls pointed to girls' desire to be liked for who they are, and they also recognized the support girls give each other. However, girls made it clear that girls are ultimately the ones who must say yay or nay to the sexual advances of boys, and they saw this as a covert form of exercising power. Overall, girls expressed the view that boys appeared to have more overt power as demonstrated by their ability to ask for sexual favors in a forward manner and boys demonstrated a willingness to manipulate to get the female favors they want.

Romantic Relationships

Dawn: Boy trying to hook up with a girl or vice versa.
Bianca: I think it's boyfriend and girlfriend. (Massachusetts: Romney)

Romantic relationships, meaning the desire for one-to-one intimate connections with another, were central to girls' thinking about why sexting occurred. The cluster of associations related to sexting and relationships illustrated how sexting could be intertwined with multiple phases of a relationship, from identification of a potential romantic interest and exploration of the relationship to a means of sustaining and expressing the relationship. Thus, sexting can be part of romantic expression in all its forms.

> Amanda: ... I guess, to eventually possibly have sex with somebody. Have a romantic relationship with them outside of technology. (South Carolina: Wes)

For relationships where distance and transportation is a factor, sexually tinged encounters by phone or Internet can serve as a kind of relationship glue.

> Gardenia: I think it's very common, because like they probably, I guess, I don't know why people do it, but I think people do it because they don't get to see the person, so they just forward pictures. (South Carolina: Brad)

Girls' discussions of romantic encounters provided many illustrations of their understanding of gendered positioning. The four girls from Massachusetts speaking here painted a complicated picture of sexual, emotional, and physical desires and the ways these may intersect with the act of sending a sexually descriptive text or image to another in the course of a relationship.

> Chau: Well, I guess it's like—if—like Daniella was saying earlier. Like if a boy or a girl is talking to someone else and then they're talking and they really like them and then they are pressured or asked to send a picture and they have a feeling like if they don't then the person will stop liking them or stop talking to them and they don't want to like have that stop ...
>
> Daniella: Also, girls can sometimes feel very self-conscious and boys have like that power. They'll be like, "Oh, no, I think you're beautiful. Especially if you like send me that picture." And they'll make a girl of self-conscious, a girl feels so good about herself that she wants to keep sending the boy pictures so then he can give her more compliments ...
>
> Anh: It's about feeling accepted and reassured about yourself ...
>
> Halina: Maybe the girl might like a guy and then the guy's like—I don't know how to put this. He's seeing another girl. Like

> they're talking. They're probably dating each other and then she sees him with another and then her friends are like, "Oh, if you want to keep your man you have to do this and this and this. If not, he's going to leave you," blah, blah. And then she's all going to be like, "Oh, maybe I should do that." ... Blah, blah, blah. And then she does it. (Massachusetts: Gateway City)

These Massachusetts girls indicated that boys, as the objects of desire and dispensers of sexual compliments, hold a certain power over them. Sexting was one means, among many communicative approaches, by which one signals desire and seeks to maintain attention and ward off other comers. As this passage suggests, the negotiations occur within couples, but also extend to one's most trusted group of peers.

The general theme of impressing or keeping a guy was referenced many times in all the discussions we held with girls.

> Hannah: I think also to impress their boyfriend ... just to get his attention again ...
> Farrah: Well, if they were talking about like married couples doing it, like if they were going to be like gone for a long time, like you had like an Army husband or something, they might do it for like a little moment, like a little keepsake of what they left back at home—I guess would be the word for it. But I also think the main reason people do it—like girls do it is because they're trying to impress a guy or they're trying to get a guy to stay with them or like something that's really insecure. (Ohio: Native)

When the discussion with girls shifted from girls' thoughts on girls' motivations for sexting to girls' thoughts on boys' motivations for sexting, the tone of the conversation took a darker turn. Girls overwhelmingly stated that boys ask girls for sexual photos far more often than the other way around. Moreover, some boys may send sexual photos to girls without any request to do so. In these cases boys may be using a sexual photograph to interest a girl in having sex by letting her see what she would be getting if she were to have sex with him.

Girls suggested that boys initiate, but it is girls who must set the limits. In the complex relationship interactions in which sexting becomes embedded, saying yes to sexting may be a way of saying no to actual sex. Not all boys, however, accept that rationale and some may use the compensation photograph as payback for no sex.

> Alma: Yes. Guys are very conniving, and mischievous. And if you do something to them, or say something to them, so they'll like try

> to start rumors about you, or if they know something about you, or stuff like that. Guys are just—ah, I hate guys. But anyways, but yeah, like if you tell them no, like, say they were to ask you for sex, and you said no, they would be like oh well, she did this with this person, and like, that's how rumors start.
> Interviewer: OK. So boys could use sexting to hurt girls?
> Alma: Yes.
> Interviewer: OK. By spreading rumors …
> Alma: Or showing the pictures.
> Breechelle: … one person, and it ends up in millions. (South Carolina: Make-Up Group)

Thus, while relationship may be a term that implies peacefulness and harmony to many, these discussions with teen girls demonstrated that within the context of relationship, sexting can serve as aggravation, retribution, and blackmail. Thwarted desires, male competitiveness, changing relationships among couples, and peer pressures were all possible motivations for using sexting in ways that have a negative impact on what one had hoped would be a trusting, intimate relationship.

Peers: Social Status, Power, and Control

While romantic relationship may be paramount to girls in their motivations for sexting, they also indicated that sexting is embedded in critical social negotiations within their world. After all, one-on-one relationships are both a private and public concern—private as they are established between a couple, but public as that relationship is recognized by their social world and its shifting concerns in regard to social status, power, and control.

As discussions with girls shifted from 'what is sexting' to 'why do people sext,' associations related to peers, power, and status increased significantly in girls' responses.

Sexting was seen as a powerful tool to assist young women in their bids for affirmation or inclusion from peers, as well as having the potential to destroy their social lives. In this regard, sexting may be one way to signal one's experience and maturity. Particularly for younger girls entering the social scene, sexting may seem like a reasonable path to looking more mature and impressing older boys.

> Becky: I was going to say that it's for the younger kids they want to be so grown up and they think that if they do that then it makes them on the same level as 17 and 18 year olds because they think that older kids just sit there all day long and sext. (Laughter) So I

> think it's like when they're younger they go oh, these other girls are too afraid to do it but I'm so grown up and mature that I can do it. I think they just do it to act older but they don't realize that they just look stupid doing it. (Massachusetts: Andrew)

Indeed, in some youth circles sexting is perceived as an act of bravery, a kind of rite of passage, signalling that you are ready to join a more prestigious group within your social world.

> Chantel: It depends on the people who you hang around. It depends on the crowd of girls and the crowd of boys you hang around. Because some girls actually may start it and be like watch I get this because of this and guys will say watch I get this because of this. And they'll be like girl, you got that, I got that too. I think it's kind of like a popularity contest for who can get the most text messages from this boy, who can get the most text messages from this girl. (South Carolina: Norton)

Girls demonstrated that competition within specific peer groups can be intense, and sexual images can be a means to increase status and put forward claims for greater attention or higher ranking within the peer group.

> Kieu: I feel like yeah, like a lot of what I say is going to tie in with like confidence and stuff, but definitely competition, because a lot of girls you know, if you like get—like there's, you know, a list going on, you know [a] list, so you're like seeing this girl all the time, this girl is hot, and then you know, you might think to yourself you know like oh, I'm way hotter than her, so I'm going to take a picture of myself provocatively and post it, or send it to people via sexting. And then you know, it's a competition. (Ohio: Norse)

While girls were reluctant to identify negative sexting incidents as bullying, they described incidents where sexting was used in ways that were explicitly designed to cause harm to others, as this passage from Brandi in South Carolina reveals.

> Brandi: I think they both may feel the same way, and try to ruin something else for somebody else. Probably because of jealousy.
> Interviewer: Ruin—OK. And by ruin and something, what would you mean?
> Brandi: Like, their reputation, or just their personality, or who they are. (South Carolina: Wes)

Girls drew sharp distinctions between girls' motivations to engage in sexting and those of boys. Boys' involvement in sexting, girls believed, would be more likely to include the motivations of bragging, strutting, displaying, gathering trophies, and even betting.

Breanna in Ohio compared boys' social and competitive drives in regard to sexting with girls' reticence and relationship concerns, demonstrating how interpretations differ based on gendered perspectives.

> Breanna: I think that like sometimes, they just think they're like so awesome with their parts. And they're just really like cocky about it, and they're like oh, I'm going to show this off to everybody 'cause I'm cool. And it's like you're not. Like that doesn't make you cool. I don't know. Just they're really cocky. I think the difference is guys are cocky about sending stuff, and that's why they send it. But girls send it out of like I don't know, like self-image issues. And when they send it, they're like nervous about sending it. So I guess that's kind of what makes the reaction different. Like girls are like wow, you're cool, but guys are like oh my God, I barely got her to send this, so it's like that much more (pause)—I don't know what the word is, but yeah. You get what I mean. (laughter) (Ohio: Astro)

Girls believed boys' competitive drive contains diverse components including competition for a specific female, for multiple females, for trophies of their conquest of females, and for ranking among other males. Girls stated male competition with males is as much about comparison of physical attributes from six-pack abs to the size of one's genitals as it is about securing females' attention or favors.

Girls suggested that this kind of sexually competitive behavior among boys happens with or without sexting. Thus, sexting is just one way to extend a kind of activity that will be happening among boys regardless of the technologies present.

> Gardenia: Most boys … show it right there in front of everybody.
> Interviewer: Is that sexting?
> ?: Flashing somebody, I don't know [if] it's sexting, but just showing your ding a ding …
> Breelyn: Mooning.
> Interviewer: OK, so Breelyn says that's not sexting, is that right?
> Breelyn: It's mooning.
> Interviewer: Mooning, OK what does Ernestine think?

Ernestine: I actually have a question. What is it with these boys who in front of they cousins or they brothers and they just like to see who (laughter) …

?: They do it in front of girls as well. (South Carolina: Brad)

Highly attuned to the forms and nuances of boys' competitive concerns, one group of girls identified betting as a component within the range of inter-related competitive activities in which sexting was embedded.

Chantel: Money.

Interviewer: Money? How do you get money?

Chantel: I guess guys bet. They make like bets that they can get this and girls can say this so they get money from betting.

Interviewer: Like among their friends or is this like a bigger thing?

Chantel: They can bet all over. They can bet with teachers and friends and family members. Bet on anybody. Anyone off the street, in a bar or something. (South Carolina: Norton)

Thus, in some communities the outcomes of sexting become part of a monetary system of exchanges that confers financial value on that competition.

Sexuality

By its very nature, questions about sexting raise issues of sexuality. Girls debated as to whether or not sexting actually was sex. They wondered if you had to be sharing naked images for it to be considered sexting. This section from a focus group in Massachusetts illustrates the questioning and debate with which young women approached this discussion.

Faith: It is safe sex, but at the same time, it's not. Like it's—anything to do with sex, it's just having a picture, it's not like you're doing anything with someone. You're trusting them with a lot, though. That's something that normally, if you're going to trust someone that much, you usually would just hook up with them, or—and do stuff with them, you wouldn't just send a picture …

Dawn: It's not like physical—I don't know if physical is the word to use, 'cause obviously if it's a picture, that's physical—but it's not like one-to-one contact, you know what I mean, like that's what really sex is, like, so, that's just sending pictures, and the guy doing what he wants to do with the pictures, I guess. (laughs) I don't know. (Massachusetts: Romney)

An interesting theme that arose in this phase of the discussion and continued in different veins was the notion of sexting as a means of avoiding intercourse. The desire to avoid actual intercourse can be related to emotional concerns, such as 'I'm not sure if I am ready' or 'I am afraid to have sex yet.'

> Chantel: [I] feel that it's through ages, I would say 13 to 18 that's really doing it. Because younger kids don't really know about it but the older kids, they don't have to send messages, they can go do it … and the kids between the ages of 13 and 18 are afraid to do it so they're going to send messages and text messages to tell them what they want to do but not physically wanting to do it. That's what [I] feel. (South Carolina: Norton)

Avoiding intercourse also addresses the more practical concerns of pregnancy and sexually transmitted diseases.

Sexting was also recognized as a potential outcome when infatuation simply carried a person away.

It is interesting to note that girls in Massachusetts and Ohio were generally more veiled in their discussion of the issue of girls' sexual desire, choosing to discuss it in terms of liking or wanting a guy or hooking up with a male. Girls in South Carolina were decidedly more explicit about girls' sexual desire as demonstrated in this exuberant, humorous, and poetic passage.

> Indigo: Maybe they just want to have sex.
> Ernestine: You may be in the mood to talk about the specific thing.
> ? : Just need that right there (inaudible).
> ? : Want right then and there, [need] to get off work, man I need this right now man.
> ? : Can't hold back, gotta let loose.
> ? : … you got this urge.
> ? : You gotta let loose.
> ? : You can't be like, oh stop. Gotta let loose. Let loose and let go.
> Ernestine: Same time, y'all saying you can't stop your hormones, but all y'all got opinions, you can control yourself. If you don't want to text (inaudible) then you don't have to.
> Indigo: To pick up on what Ernestine was saying, like you may be in that mood right then, but then say it might come back to haunt you, like you're in that mood then and you send it. Then something happens and it get out then everybody know your business. (South Carolina: Brad)

SEXTING: MORAL EVALUATIONS AND DANGERS

Girls' moral evaluations of sexting varied considerably. Many girls pointed to a lack of self-confidence or a need for self-esteem as powering girls' involvement in sexting. Heather's comment is typical of these concerns.

> Heather: Oh. I most definitely feel like it is to get like attention, and if you feel like you're unwanted, like people are going to be like well, and they build up, it'll build up. Like it might not initially be like this, like that, but like one thing leads to another, and then you're like oh, it's passed. (Ohio: Norse)

Girls' sexting behavior was connected in some cases to an individual's home background. Heather, above, referenced this generally, but Bonnie below makes specific reference to the lack of a mother's input, which was similar to other more specific references. Such references may indicate an underlying social belief shared widely within our culture that mothers are responsible for the moral values of a daughter.

> Bonnie: I feel like it doesn't matter what age you are when it comes to sexting. It like depends on how you was raised. Like if you're brought up when your mama will talk to you about stuff like that then you wouldn't really sext. But if your mama ain't talked to you like that and then teach you stuff, you know like that, then you will be out there. It's like most of the kids, like the girls, the little fast girls and stuff like that. (South Carolina: Norton)

Teens tended not to use the term sexting, preferring to talk about actual practices such as forwarding and sharing. This constraint against using the term sexting changed as they shifted to discuss the realm of the dangerous and, in particular, to the issue of outside sexual predators. Teens were aware of the significant dangers of predators, and they were not eager to encounter such folk. Tales of pedophiles, blackmailers, and others lurked in their minds like urban legends. The teens we spoke with had no desire to seek out such involvement and appeared to shun those who would do so.

When talking about the point where forwarding and sharing crossed over into sexting, two pivotal characteristics were: 1) public broadcasting and 2) pornography. Girls identified pornography as sexually exploitive, dirty, and unacceptable. They pointed out that boys are more likely to seek out pornography than girls.

> Indigo: The only way I see it as a positive is if you're [in] a career aspiring to be a stripper or working in porno ... (South Carolina, Brad)

LAYERS OF SHAME: THE CONSEQUENCES OF SEXTING FROM GIRLS' PERSPECTIVES

Girls were acutely aware of the personal dangers that attend sexting, and for girls, the personal, social, and emotional consequences appeared to far outweigh the legal or economic consequences.

The terms slut and whore arose frequently in focus group interviews when speaking of girls who were publicly revealed as engaging in sexting. These negative terms were applied specifically to girls, and no such parallel term appeared to exist for boys.

> Amanda: Negative reasons – first off, if the person that is receiving the text message gets caught with it, they're going to get in trouble, while the person that sends the text message, they're going to get in trouble. Probably your reputation is not going to be what you want it to be. You'll get that label of "easy," or "slut," whatever. (South Carolina: Wes)
>
> Gloria: Phoebe Prince, I think she sent her boyfriend a picture or something and then like he spread it around ... And then like the whole school found out and they were calling her like slut and racist things ... They were just like bullying around that. (Massachusetts: Gateway City)

As these girls illustrate, being labelled in this way brings down harsh consequences on a girl, including widespread social condemnation.

Girls were strongly aware that boys do not face similar moral negatives for their involvement in sexting.

> Bethany: I feel like guys, it's another one of those things where it's like a double standard, like if girls have sex with a bunch of dudes, they're a ho [whore], but if guys have sex with a bunch of girls, like oh, I got it in with this girl, this girl, this girl, then you're cool, like oh man, you're a pimp. You know, like I—it's such a double standard, and guys want to be able to do it so they can brag and be like yeah man, I get hos. Guys respect that, and girls don't. (Ohio: Astro)

As bad as peer shaming of a girl, girls were also deeply fearful of the shame they would face from their family.

> Breanna: I think it all depends on like what kind of parents you have. 'Cause like I've talked to my mom before about like various things, and she's like (pause) Breanna ... like I'll remember that for the rest of your—Like my mom doesn't really give me

"redemption." Like if I do something wrong that's as big as sexting, like she will remember it. Like she's not one to forgive and forget. She's one to forgive, and remember. (laughter) So it just depends on what your parents are like. (Ohio: Astro)

A girl who engaged in sexting would not only face shame from her own family, but would bring shame upon her family.

Denise: I think parents are going to be really judgmental. Like right away off the bat, I think they're going to be like oh, like we're more, yeah we judge people I [know] they do it. But we're like whatever, like we're their age, we understand. Like yeah, that was gross, like you're a gross person. We understand like why you did it, like I don't know. But parents, they're just like oh my gosh, like why'd they do that? And then they might judge their parents, or like they might just like not let you hang out with their kid, even though their kid might not be a bad person and stuff like that.

Carolyn: That's exactly what I was going to say. They're going to have like a reputation from all the adults that they're not going to want their kids hanging out around them because of it. (Ohio: Astro)

Girls recognized that they can be unfairly labelled by others and then forced unfairly to live with shame.

Candace: ... And when you're not respecting yourself, the person you send it to, they're going to disrespect you, like if you do something they don't like, like, oh, do you want to hang out, oh no, I'm busy, and then like, you keep avoiding them or something, like, they could do something like turn on you, and it's like, oh, well, whatever, she's a slut, blah blah blah, and like, he can like, send your picture to everybody. Yeah. And that's not something that a girl or a boy would want to happen. That's how rumors start. (Massachusetts: Romney)

Girls were highly aware that they are in double jeopardy in regard to this labelling and shaming process because of their gender as well as their designation as an adolescent who has not reached the legal age of consent.

Gabrielle: If you think about it, it would make more sense for older people to do it because at our age you get looked at as like a slut or like a whore but if you're older it's kind of like, whatever, like

I'm old enough to do what I want to do. (Massachusetts: Andrews)

The shame that girls described as a consequence of public revelation of sexting behavior was like the head of Medusa with its many snarled snakes for hair. The shamed are vile and not to be looked upon, as one glance can turn others to stone.

WHO WILL GUIDE GIRLS THROUGH THESE DANGEROUS WATERS?

Optimally, teen girls have two primary sources of adult input in dealing with these issues: 1) adults within their family; and 2) adults within their school. In our sample, there was little discussion of significant adult others outside of these spheres.

Adults in the Family

Girls perceived parents to be generally uncomfortable with topics of this sort, and whether this was cause or consequence, girls were also uncomfortable discussing these topics with their parents.

> Amanda: I think it's non-existent, pretty much. Parents sometimes live in denial. And most children don't feel comfortable enough to talk with their parents. So I don't really think it's a conversation that most typical families have. (South Carolina: Wes)

Girls emphasized that the ability to talk to a parent is related to the quality of the relationship between girl and parent. They believed many factors could influence a parent's involvement or perceptions.

> Elena: I think it depends on the relationship that the child has with the adult and how the adult was raised. If you have a really close relationship with the adult and they're more open than other adults would be I think they would be more like accepting of it. Where an adult who was raised without cell phones or without technology and their parents were really strict, they would be like oh my god, stop. (Massachusetts: Andrews)

Teen girls feared negative parent reactions and mentioned many forms that this could take, from parents who would take legal matters into their own hands or withdraw trust from a young person, to those who would share their anger or chagrin with other family or community members, widening the circle of shame and distrust in which the young person was thrust.

Despite concerns about communication and trust, girls still turned to parents as the first port of call when seeking protection from threatening behaviors.

> Dawn: Or, like, back to the parents, they would, like if someone kept sending them pictures, like, daily or whatever, and like, they kept asking them to stop, and they wouldn't stop, then like—if that happened to me, like, I'd definitely tell my mom, be like, get this creep away from me. (Massachusetts: Romney)

Adults in School

Girls suggested that few educators would identify sexting or issues of sexuality and teen intimacy as appropriate topics for school consideration. In the experience of the majority of our participants, school adults engaged in discussion of these topics on a reactive, not a proactive basis.

Whereas teen girls portrayed parents as uncomfortable with raising the subject of sexting, they portrayed school faculty and staff as disinterested, removed, or in the worst case, as dangerous people with whom to have a conversation about the topic. Principals were described as unseen and out of the picture. Counselors, one young woman quipped, were too busy to become involved.

For the most part, girls believed school involvement around an issue like sexting would fall on the shoulders of teachers. Girls, however, expressed many doubts in regard to speaking with teachers, including concerns that teachers were not interested in the personal lives of their students, or that they would prove untrustworthy confidants, sharing private information widely with others. Girls were aware that mandated reporting on issues like sexting ties the hands of many school officials. Most of our participants had little confidence that sexting would be addressed in health class, which they saw as more focused on concerns about health and well-being, that is, topics like nutrition and exercise and the dangers of alcohol and drugs.

> Alma: I think, like if a counselor is fine ... you're doing it, they'll try to talk to you about it, but it's like, you don't really know me, so why am I talking to you if I don't know you ... That's exactly like administrators, or like your teachers. Yeah, you see me in school, but other than that, you don't know me, you don't know what I like to do.
>
> Breechelle: Yes, that's so true. [laughter] ... I mean, teachers try to get all close to me. I mean, it's nice for a teacher to act like they

care, and it's nice and all of that good stuff, but I mean, uh-uh.
[laughter] (South Carolina: Make-up Group)

The one tool youth seemed to use to bring the discussion forward was that of joking or humor. In this context, they could touch on a subject that appeared to have great danger for young people and the adults who work with them.

Girls indicated that adults' issues with sexting were intertwined with the problems they were having, overall, with the technological age.

> Gardenia: I think, schools in general like, they do, by them blocking certain websites, they're blocking how we can like do research papers and stuff like that, because they have everything blocked. We can only go on certain websites. But at the same time, like it's a good thing that you're blocking these sites, but at the same time, it's a bad thing, because you cutting off education resources as well. (South Carolina: Brad)

It is important to note that girls presented very different pictures of school and the possibility of genuine relationships with teachers depending on the region of the United States in which they were located. Girls in the Midwest seemed to have the most trusting relationships with educators.

THE ROLE OF THE MEDIA

Girls were strongly aware of the media (meaning broadcasting, cable, and related components of the media industry) as a force informing them about sexuality in general, and sexting in particular.

Sexting was a theme on many popular teen shows that girls mentioned. In addition to *Degrassi High*, mentioned below, teen girls also referred to *High School Musical* and *Glee*.

> Gloria: I watched an episode of *Degrassi* and this girl sent her boyfriend a picture and then they found out, like the school found out about it. They're like, "Oh, you can be like charged for like child pornography, for distribution of child pornography." I've seen that a lot. (Massachusetts: Gateway City)

Interestingly, girls mentioned daytime talk shows, more than any other group interviewed, as a place where they learned about issues related to sexting. These included *Dr. Phil*, *Jerry Springer*, *The Maury Povitch Show*, *Montel*, *Nancy Grace*, and *The Tyra Banks Show*, among others.

Teen girls were strongly aware of celebrities and their involvement in sexting.

Daniella: Also, yeah, I agree the media, especially with celebrities. Celebrities are a role model to young people, so whatever they do teens will want to reoccur. Like their actions. (Massachusetts: Gateway City)

GIRLS' LIVES IN THESE CHANGING TIMES

Girls saw themselves as living in a time of dramatic change. They recognized the vast gulf that is emerging between themselves as teens and adults. They pointed to changes in sexual and ethical practices, as well as changes in technology. Adults, they believed, are vastly uncomfortable with these changes and are struggling to make sense of them.

Girls were quick to point out the double standard they feel exists, where teens are criticized for doing things that adults may be doing themselves. Teens are growing up to become individuals capable of sexual and intimate expression, and at what point do they cross that line between irresponsible and responsible?

In keeping with the theme of changing times, girls pointed out how photographs and digital phones are making their way into new scenarios of romance and involvement. In this new world, sharing phones is an accepted practice. There is a new etiquette of relationships evolving in which, for instance, you clean your phone of couple photos when you break up.

While many teen girls thought of sexting as common or unremarkable, they also pointed out that teens hold a variety of opinions on the topic, just as do adults. They cautioned against painting all teens with the same brush.

Through the lens of discussions on sexting, teen girls demonstrated the strong hold traditional gender roles still play in their personal, familial, and social lives. In these conversations with young women from three regions of the United States, males were depicted as sexually more aggressive—more likely to ask for photos and to seek photos for bragging rights. Girls, on the other hand, were depicted as holding the line through negotiating no to sexual involvement. In incidents of sexting gone wrong, girls faced multiple layers of personal shame including the shame they bring on their families.

Sexting (or as teens might be more likely to say, forwarding or sharing) was not just an issue between two individuals, it was also a tool in the arsenal of young people who are striving to socially define themselves by rank and status. Girls described how sexting can be used as a means of blackmail or revenge, as well as a way of demonstrating popularity. Sexting can marginalize in one setting, or show strength and allegiance in another.

If gender is conceived as a movement turning towards or away through performances that are shaped by social contexts and spaces and the values that are embedded in them, then the girls with whom we spoke demonstrated a strong collective understanding of the status quo for the female gender as it is conceived in today's world. While the technologies they use may be new, the scenarios of sexual involvement, interaction, rewards and dangers described by these young women appear at times to share commonalities with stories of women's missteps from the Bible's *Old Testament* or the tales of Jane Austen from the early 1800s (Davidson, Thompson, & Harris, 2014). Much has changed, but much remains the same.

TEEN BOYS AND THE PHENOMENON OF SEXTING

SEXTING AND BOYS: DIVERSITY OF OPINIONS AND PRACTICES

Boys struggled to define sexting with clarity; it was an illusory target for them. The difficulties they faced in definition were multiple. First, there was a diversity of viewpoints across individuals and social groups. Boys' views of sexting ranged from 'everyone is doing it' to 'sexting is rape,' and everything in between.

Second, sexting was not a term commonly used by these youth. They were perfectly comfortable talking about forwarding, sharing, sending or receiving, but sexting was not a natural or indigenous term. As Denzel, a young man from Wes in South Carolina stated, "We don't really call it sexting, we just say—Hey! Look at this picture."

Third, the young people we spoke with identified many acts that they would associate as components of sexting, but they were hard put to create a definition of sexting from those pieces. In their eyes, sexting could include naked photos of body parts sent via cell phone, or something as simple as a sexually suggestive good night message. Moreover, from boys' perspectives, acts of sexting could be part of the beginning, middle or end of a relationship. In other words, digital tools could help you to meet someone, probe the romantic possibilities, and could also figure in the break-up of a relationship. How you use these tools depended on your perspective, the tools, your social circle, and other environmental factors.

Fourth, boys may have minimized the meaning of sexting by eliding it with more light hearted notions.

> Eloni: I think that when it comes to boys—I don't know. It's more like the fun and joking around. But, like, we just keep it in the group, like, the close friends group. Don't really—but then I don't know what sexting is. What is sexting? It's hard to … (Massachusetts: Gateway City)

Although boys held diverse opinions about sexting, it would be safe to say that Cordell represented the growing consensus among young males: sexting may not be so very strange or different than the kisses and hugs—

41

xxxooo—with which one signs a letter to a romantic partner. Sexuality and affection are sprinkled throughout their lives, and they make use of the media available to them to express those feelings.

> Cordell: I think that people get sexting. Let's say sexting, they think about these awful things, sending pictures of naked parts, or all that stuff. But sexting can be as simple as—as simple as just saying hey, you know, am I going to get some tonight? You know, something like that or yeah, that was a good kiss or something as simple as that. That sounds sexual, that's sexting. I mean it's not like you got to send a whole video of yourself, and people make it out to be some horrible thing. Everybody does it. I think everybody does it. Everybody does it. (South Carolina: Brad)

Regardless of boys' approval or disapproval of sexting, most were of the belief that sexting was common within their age group and in their schools. Despite the commonness of the practice and the understanding that it is sexual, boys struggled to explain just what kind of sex you experience with sexting and how the sexual messages are to be interpreted.

> Connor: I think it's—it's almost like you're flirting with a robot, basically. Like, that's what it's like. Because you're saying that, like, you can't see what the other person's actually feeling like when they say that to you, so you're like, you have no clue whether they're playing with your head, like, whether they're genuine about it or—you really just don't know. (Massachusetts: Romney)

Some boys, however, were careful to point out that acceptance of the notion of sexting varies by individual, age, and social group.

MOTIVATIONS PROPELLING BOYS TO SEXTING

For boys, sexting—meaning sexual encounters of the digital kind, usually at some distance from the other party—was embedded within four concerns. The first three concerns were sex, peer social relationships, and romance or intimate relationships. Finally, a fourth and interesting addition to boys' motivations for sexting was the influence of the media.

The order of concerns may vary by individual, but it is safe to say that boys frequently pointed first to sex and peer social relationships as motivators. The reason they did so may be that they were more comfortable taking up the discussion of these topics. Romance and a desire for individual intimacy were certainly of interest to them, but they did not privilege it above the others. Indeed, boys noted that, in contrast to themselves, the search for a one-on-one enduring relationship was a strong motivator for girls who might sext.

> Abraham: Because it's like, they want a relationship, they don't want to be known as oh that guy hooked up with her, and this guy hooked up with me, so no, he's afraid to hook up with me now. And you have sometimes, when guys want to like put their friend down with the girl they just hooked up with. So, it's like, the girls want more of a relationship. (South Carolina: Make-Up Group)

Sex

In contrast to girls' described reticence about sex, boys were more likely to respond, "I mean a lot of guys, they don't really care" (Ford at Astro in Ohio); "Guys are probably more sexually driven" (Brad at Wes in South Carolina); or "Guys think about sex." (Cleveland also at Wes in South Carolina)

Boys spoke in some detail of the ways sexting can bring satisfaction to the male participant. For instance, as one participant described, if you have never seen someone naked, sexting would be an opportunity to see what is underneath the clothing. Sexting can provide you with the chance to get aroused and to arouse the other.

Sexting can also be a milestone on the path to a full sexual encounter.

> Cleveland: They will show the body, but they won't actually do it until they're really, fully prepared to do it. (South Carolina, Wes)

Some boys believed that showing their body parts could induce sexual interest in girls, leading to greater likelihood of sexual fulfilment.

> Cordell: Just guys mainly do it. Just I guess like he said earlier ... lure the girl in. [T]here's only so much you could say or text to a girl, you know? But if she actually sees it, she'll be more likely to give it up. (South Carolina: Brad)

Thus, sexual display was connected, in boys' minds, to sexual enticement.

Boys were also aware of the safety benefits of sexting over actual intercourse, from concerns about pregnancy to the prevention of sexually transmitted diseases.

Dillon: I think they think that they're really unlikely to get caught doing it, and think it's a lot more risk-free than actually having sex. (Ohio: Astro)

For the boys we spoke with, sexting was embedded in the complex dance of sexual intimacy. Such encounters were worked out through time-honored genres that roamed from curiosity and identification of a potential partner to teasing, flirting, and testing, to various levels of trusting and sexual acts.

Peers, Social Relations, and Power

For boys, the practices associated with sexting were connected in many ways to peer social relations and the exercise of power within the peer group. Boys openly discussed the ways they compete and how sexting activities became part of these competitions.

Competitiveness can take several forms in regard to sexting. First, it can be a way to demonstrate a boy's ability to acquire sexual photos from girls. Sexual photos acquired from girls can be compared by overall number of photos or by the ability to receive sexual photos from girls who are deemed desirable by the social group.

Abraham: Just because they want to say that they got one of the hottest girls. It's like a competition with guys." (South Carolina: Make-up group)

In this sense, acquiring a photo token of a particular girl's attention added social capital to the receiving male's account.

Frederick: I agree with … Clayton. Sometimes it can be peer pressure. Because what if that girl is the girl that everybody wants, like, and then you get her and then you show off to your boys? "Hey! Like, brother, this is what she looks like," like. And then everybody like, "You the man," or whatever, because you got her. (Ohio: Norse)

Interestingly, while boys were ranking girls, they were aware that girls were also ranking boys, as Diondre described in this discussion of the notion of 'at least.'

Diondre: Well, my sisters always told me this: girls like a guy who has an 'at least.' So you might [say] this dude's ugly, but 'at least' he got a big—This dude's ugly but 'at least' he got a nice car … He doesn't have a job, but 'at least' he's nice looking. She said a guy always has to have an 'at least' no matter what. And if you don't have nothing, then ... (South Carolina: Brad)

Of particular concern among boys in the competition for ranking—by boys and girls—was the size of the penis, alternately described by our participants as 'your package,' 'what you are packing,' 'Johnson,' or 'it.'

Elijah: But a lot of times, when people are insecure about certain things, they constantly try to prove otherwise, and trying to prove other people wrong and trying to prove it to themselves that they're not like that, or do certain things. They're trying to prove the opposite of what's really true. So like with your example of the dude who's small and you're saying like he won't send a picture of it, yeah, but he's probably going to send a different angle or something ... (Ohio: Norse)

Boys described the many ways pressures to belong, to shine, and to achieve social rank could be acted out through sexting practices. Sexting could be seen as a means of joining a certain social crowd, looking cool, or fitting in.

Clayton: [It is] ... kind of like, if you don't do it, then you're like scared—be like scared to do it. (Ohio, Norse)

For boys a significant issue in regard to competing for the attention of girls was that they are outranked by older boys or men. Boys saw girls' attraction to older males as a significant reason girls may find themselves in trouble with sexting. As Cleveland, a young man from Wes in South Carolina stated, "... girls like to date older guys, so they [older guys] might convince them [girls] to do something."

Romantic Relationships

Aaron: ... I feel like if you're being romantic with someone, then it's not sexting, because I feel like sexting's more like 'show me your body.' But romantic isn't exactly sexting. And I don't really feel like you can mix the two very much, and if you are mixing the two, then it's more sexting than not ... (Romney, MA)

As described earlier, boys possessed diverse views of sexting and the motivations that prompt people to engage in it. The desire to press forward in a romantic relationship was among the primary motivations for boys' sexting behaviors, but boys may interpret the role of sexting in that relationship in different ways. Aaron, above, drew a psychological line between sexting and romance, arguing that if you really care for the other person, the exchange of sexual photos is not an act of sexting.

Other boys described a more literal divide between sexting and romantic relationships, declaring that one would not sext in a romantic relationship out of respect for the other person.

> Elijah: I disagree. I don't think it happens so often in romantic relationships. I think it happens more in like lustful relationships. Because in romantic relationships sex isn't so in the forefront ... I mean, it is a big topic but it's not so in the forefron ... like with lustful relationships, when people were just trying to have sex.
>
> Clayton: Yeah, I would like to agree with Elijah ... [L]ike he said [in] relationships, you like respect the person more. So, you know, you wouldn't treat them like that. (Ohio: Norse)

Still others negotiated a place for sexting in the romance. In these cases, sexting was present because of romantic interest and the trust that builds through romantic engagement leads a couple to sext.

> Fritz: I feel like, typically, there's some form of romantic involvement before any of this starts. It may not have been anything physical, but they have been talking about doing something, or living together at some point, and that's how the sort of window opens up for the trust to begin, which is when they start sending pictures, because they don't think that anything's going to happen to them, because they trust the other person that they're talking to ... The other person may be a trustworthy person, and it may be a part of your relationship, depending on who you are, and what you do, but I feel like, typically in most cases, it sprouts from some form of romantic involvement, no matter how deep. (Massachusetts: Andrews)

While the desire to enter a romantic relationship can be a prompt for boys' sexting, as a romance ends sexting may play a role. The anger of a break-up can lead to the use of the once-cherished sexual photos as a tool for revenge.

> Ebisu: [A]nother way you'd get it out to other people, is like they break up, or they start disliking each other. Oh I don't like you, so to the Internet you go ... [Y]ou're trying to hurt the person's feelings ... You might not think of it afterwards, you're like, oh I really didn't need to do that out of pure anger, but it's just, you're doing it because the relationship is over, and you're angry. (Massachusetts: Andrews)

46

The discussion of boys' views of sexting motivators was peppered with references to boys' notions of inherency, that is, their views of what is inherent to boys' or girls' nature. For instance, in talking about sex as a motivator for sexting, boys declared their overt interest in this topic. They believed that this interest is inherent to their gendered identity, whether that is biological or social. When boys act in ways inconsistent with the norms of inherency, their gender identification is called into question.

Media as a Motivator for Sexting

Teen boys produced both classical and new arguments for us in regard to how the media might be motivating young males to engage in sexting. The classical viewpoint was offered by Ford and Ezra in Ohio, who pointed to the attention celebrities glean from sexting and how this provides a model for young people.

> Ford: I feel like celebrities help out on that. Like, they show, like, TV shows, whatever, there are a lot of sexual scenes, and, like, it shows that, like—it makes it look like sex is OK or being sexy is OK. And a part or in a way it is, but not, like, sending pictures ...
> Ezra: ... off of what Ford said, it's like, how we've had these huge, like, three or four scandals with sexting [in] this past, like, week, so I think that the kids see that, and they're like, "Well, if these guys are doing it, and look how much attention ..." As Alan said, you know, "let me do it, and I'll get attention," you know. If movie stars are doing it and I want to be a movie star, then why can't I do it? So, I think motivation comes from the older people. (Ohio, Astro)

As Ford, Ezra (and Alan) illustrated, in their search for information about how to be liked and accepted boys take note of the messages the media offers on these topics.

The boys we spoke with also offered more subtle reflections on the ways the media may be modelling values about sexuality and providing suggestions for behavior to which boys are paying attention.

> Derek: I think the media has a huge influence on sexting. Because, like, almost every pop song is about girls and whatnot. And everyone hears that, and you hear it so much, you want to start being like that. I mean, and that's why bands, like other bands, like Green Day, like Some 41, that's why they're so acclaimed and so good. Because they're not singing about relationships and having girlfriends: they're singing about being a kid and being a

47

> punk, like, punky, screwed-up—like, they don't care. They're
> singing about bad relationships and girls messing with them and
> just doing stupid stuff that you do as a kid …
>
> Frank: Well, the way college is portrayed, too, to a lot of kids, is
> you're going to go through and you're eventually going to get
> your degree, but you're going to party. And a lot of movies, too
> … the theme is you wake up the next morning wondering what
> just happened. It's in a lot of music videos, too. And like Derek
> said, it's in a lot of entertainment and media, I think.
> (Massachusetts, Romney)

In this version of the media as motivator, boys described the heavy
emphasis the media places on gendered relationships—girls to boys and
vice versa. This emphasis can be seen in songs and bands, movies, TV,
music videos, and other entertainment and media. The message the media is
conveying, boys suggested, places huge emphasis on sexual relationships
and boy-girl interactions. They described how boys are drawn to the
realistic portrayals of teen life—its grubbiness and failures—but are also
subconsciously affected by the subtext about a lifestyle where you "wake
up the next morning wondering what just happened."

CONSEQUENCES FROM A BOY'S POINT OF VIEW

Boys' perspectives on the consequences of sexting were shaped by the
gendered position from which they were located. For instance, boys
believed they are less vulnerable to the pressures of sexting than girls
because they simply care less about having their photos exposed. Boys said
that a boy who believes himself to have been bullied by a girl to send a
photo is an "idiot" (South Carolina: Brad).

In tandem with boys' lessened sense of vulnerability to sexting, boys saw
girls as more vulnerable to sexting and less able to fend off boys' pressure
to engage in sexting. Boys, however, did not regard the pressure they apply
to girls to sext as bullying because they view the pressure as a request not a
threat.

> Antoine: No, I don't think it would be pressure or bullying. I think it's
> —you know what you're doing, so it really isn't pressure or
> bullying. (South Carolina: Norton)

Whereas girls who are publicly exposed for engaging in sexting may be
labelled terms that convey deep shame, such as slut, whore, or flip (see the
following section), boys recognized that similar labels are not applied to
them. Interestingly, boys might apply the term slut or whore to themselves

(as in speaking of a boy who is promiscuous), but these were isolated incidents. It was more likely that they may receive encouragement or praise from peers or others for their actions. In this sense, boys had an overall awareness of the gendered double standard in operation in regard to sexting.

> Ade: It's kind of two-sided. That's why, that's like, at the beginning of the discussion, we were saying, it's usually the girl sending, and the guy trying to talk the girl into sending, because girls usually they know the status that comes with it, if it gets out. And guys like … who knows, it's a probably good status. (South Carolina: Wes)

Boys believed girls' vulnerability means that they may be more likely to cause harm to themselves as a result of exposure for a sexting incident.

> Eloni: I think that sexting can lead to, like, suicide of, like, the victim … They can, like, feel so bad about it. Like, everyone knowing about what they—I don't know, what they do about that … Yeah, it got around somehow and then that's—I guess that's kind of like bullying … The girl can like—suicide or something. (Massachusetts: Gateway City)

In contrast, a consequence boys might face is the loss of status through sexual engagement with what their social group considers ugly girls, as this extended passage illustrates:

> Diondre: I mean there's a lot of things you can get from having sex with a girl. If you have sex with a lot of girls, then you're the man on campus. If you have sex with this pretty girl, then you're the man on campus. You can't have sex with too many ugly girls. I mean, sex is sex. We all know that you're getting some, you're getting some. But if you have sex with ugly girls when they have sex with pretty girls, then it's frowned upon …
> Interviewer: What do you call a guy that has sex with a lot of ugly girls? Is there a name, kind of like a flip?
> Cordell: Idiot. We call them idiot.
> Diondre: It could be a lemon or a busted lover … loser. (South Carolina: Brad)

While boys perceived the personal consequences of their sexual engagement, including sexting, to be different than those for girls, they were also aware that boys face different consequences from parents for their sexual entanglements with girls. These differences were present in the reactions of their own parents, the parents of the girl, and from any other parents aware of the activity. The complexity of boy-girl-parent interactions are revealed in this passage:

> Brad: I was going to say that girls are probably more prone to doing this, than guys are. Girls probably send more, than guys do, but only because a girl, you know, it's kind of hard, I'm guessing, obviously I'm not a girl, I'm guessing would be kind of harder for a girl to get out of the house. Because with parents, they're thinking, oh that's my little girl. With some parents, they're like oh that's my little boy, nothing bad is really going to happen to him, but that same parent, you know, you got a little girl, you're like, hey my teenage boy can go do this, but my teenage girl can't go do this, because she might get hurt ... or something like that. Parents are definitely against it, but I think that more females would probably try to do this, just to see if they can get away with it, so that way they can get something out of it, but they're probably more scared to do it, because there's more they can lose. Like if their parents did find out, their parents would be upset, stuff like that. But say they send it, and one of their friends get it, and then one of their friends is a good friend of the parent. That's a good way to get in a lot of trouble, for a female. The guy gets caught, and usually the parents don't want to say, too much to them, because that's just plain awkward.
>
> Interviewer: OK. So, girls can probably get in more trouble, with their parents, than guys would.
>
> Brad: Yeah. (South Carolina: Wes)

This same group of boys also recognized that parental pressure could come from many angles.

> Cleveland: I'm going to have to say, if a son got caught sexting by his father, he'll probably be in ... [deep trouble is implied] If it's his mother, then the mother would be like, don't be disrespecting this young lady like that, by sending naked pictures to her, and don't be doing that in my house ...
>
> Denzel: Daddy's little girl, mommy's little girl.
>
> Cleveland: Yeah, they'll be like, you need to be more respectful ... boy. (South Carolina: Wes)

In both extended passages, the boys made clear that with parents, as is true among teens, a double standard exists in which girls are positioned as sexually valuable but vulnerable and boys are positioned as sexually more voracious and better able to roll with the punches. Girls, it appears, are in charge of saying no to boys' requests, and while boys are cautioned about their sexually assertive behavior, their aggressiveness in regard to sexual interests is tolerated to a large extent.

Boys had a general awareness that legal consequences exist for sexting and were able to name some of those consequences, including possession of child pornography, felony, indecent exposure, and sex offender status. These forms of legal consequences seemed to apply more to the boys than to girls, who were imagined to be in a reactive position to a sexting incident (shamed or suicidal). Boys were very aware of the legal line that divides the under 18-year-old from the over 18-year-old and the problems that would ensue from relationships between older boys and younger girls (the opposite issue, older girls and younger boys, was not raised in any of the focus groups).

That being said, it was also true that for many of the boys with whom we spoke, these legal consequences seemed surprisingly distant and vague in their conversation.

> Interviewer: So are y'all aware of any type of like legal consequences for sexting? Like pictures or the text and stuff?
> Bevaun: I was informed not too long ago that that will get you into some big trouble … Like sending nude pictures or whatever to people. 'Cause (pause) I heard about something that happened on the news one day with that—when the police tracked the little thing, and they found the pictures and stuff. And yeah, it's illegal to do that nowadays, I heard. (South Carolina: Brad)

While the media is one point of access for information about sexting, more poignant and riveting is knowledge of a sexting incident in one's school or community.

> Hugh: I don't think most people are aware of the consequences. Like, they kind of know, but they have that invincibility thought, like, "It's not going to happen to me." And you don't realize that it's the same for everybody. You can get caught for it. Like last year, at another school, somebody sent a picture and it spread around and then the police got involved and I think the person got expelled. I don't know, but it's not until things like that happen that you truly think about what could happen. (Ohio: Native)

Some young men in the focus groups felt pretty much unaware of the legal consequences to sexting.

Alaric: I had Health my freshman year and we did not talk about this so I am not aware of the consequences. But also I don't even know exactly what they constitute as sexting. So I don't know pretty much anything about it. (Ohio: Native)

Most boys generally believed penalties for sexting are too harsh and, indeed, that laws will not be able to prevent young people from sexting. Boys' rationale for this belief points back to the earlier discussion in this chapter about boys' conceptualization of sexting, not as a technological issue, but rather as a set of practices embedded in sexual expression. At the same time, an identifiable contingent of those we spoke with felt that there needed to be laws that would protect young people from dangerous adults.

Abraham: I think it's fair, because you shouldn't even be talking to a teenager if you're grown like that. If you're 32, you shouldn't be talking to a 16 year old ... You can't do stuff like that.
Interviewer: So you think that's a legitimate thing, you're okay with that type of law?
Abraham: I'm okay with that type of law. (South Carolina: Make-up Group)

GENDER, CLASS, AND SEXUALITY: THE CASE OF THE FLIP

Up to now I have sought to show how the points I am making about sexting and gender are supported by data across all three sites of the study. However, I am now going to briefly step away from that self-imposed rule to discuss the term *flip*, an issue that arose solely in South Carolina. This term was raised by boys at Brad High School in South Carolina and by girls from Norton High School in South Carolina. In both cases, the users of the terms were African-Americans. It is important to note that while the term flip appears to be indigenous to African-Americans in the South, the practices described most certainly have counterparts in different regions and among diverse racial or cultural groups.

Flip is a term that has strong resonance with slut or whore, but its meaning is more particular than those two terms. It is exclusively applied to females. Here is how Diondre from Brad in South Carolina defined it:

Diondre: I mean sexting actually like honestly, y'all agree with me, honestly at least three times—three days out of the week you'll at least get at least two and it'll be something like—it depends it's like we got these girls, we call them flips. A flip is a girl who usually—the definition of a flip is when a guy talks to a girl, he usually has sexual contact with her. It usually starts in a text. That's how you break the ice. If you say something smooth like easy about you're probably like you're trying to throw something sexual inside there. And if she bites on it, then there you got her. Then after a while you start sexting her, talking about this and that, then you have sex eventually. So then you put her onto a guy who doesn't seem—he's your friend. But when he comes into the picture, you make it seem as if you don't know him. You shut him off like a little while, he's your friend now, you shut him out, make sure the girl is you know, talking ... You give her number, give him a chance to get her number, then you give him a chance to have sex with her, and then it keeps carrying on through the whole group. And eventually the girls like we call them flips 'cause they flip from one guy inside a group to another guy. (South Carolina: Brad)

Diondre and the other participants in the group agreed that there could be school-wide, city-wide, and even nationwide flips. They asserted that girls who are labelled with this term are aware they have been designated as members of this group or social class.

Cordell: All these girls, yes they do know they're being flipped. They do. They like stuff like that. They're also—females—... that just like having sex with everybody, you know? (South Carolina: Brad)

Although this chapter focuses on description of boys' experience, it's important to know that girl participants at Norton in South Carolina corroborated the term:

Chantel: So a flip is like she'll do whatever it takes to get what she wants or what she needs. So she will do potentially whatever. (Laughter) That's what a flip is ... [It] means that she'll do this, she'll do that or she's out there, everybody knows about it, not just inside the school. Like maybe a different school may know about her or a different certain part of the street or area may know about her. So if you're called a flip it's really not a good thing. (South Carolina: Norton)

As in the boys' focus group, girls assented to the view that girls are often aware when they have been labelled flips.

While the label of flip is harsh and seemingly unredeemable, boys demonstrated some sympathetic knowledge of the circumstances that might place a girl in this position.

> Cordell: I was talking to a girl one day. She's a flip or whatever. I was like why are you – like why are you doing this? And she's like well, you know I've been through this, I've been through X, Y, and Z. I go through this at home, and sex is my only way to— you know, deal with things. That's how I feel better about it ... I found that interesting. It was like man, you know that's deep. You know, some people they use having sex with everybody as a way to—as a—like some people use sports as an outlet. They— some people study, listen to music. Some people just use sex as an outlet 'cause they've been through so much, and they feel like that's the only way they could be accepted or they could feel better about themselves. So that's why.

From an analysis of these texts, it can be seen that flip is a category positioned awkwardly between romance and prostitution—a bridge between unpaid and paid sexual work. The person who enters this category has been identified as vulnerable and groomed or seasoned to take up the sexual work of the flip. The female's vulnerable characteristics may make her appear complicit with the invitation and entry into this domain.

The practices associated with the term flip must certainly be present in other regions and within other cultural settings. For instance, think of the ways women may be victimized by male athletes within a high school or the ways girls representing different national or class backgrounds might be separated out for negative attention.

The harshness of this discussion stands in stark contrast to the more cheerful opening of the chapter where boys talk blithely about checking out a girl's photo, which they or a friend have received. As the term flip reminds us, there is a dark side to adolescent sex and the expression of gendered relationships that should not be overlooked. While young men were reluctant to think of sexting as bullying, they were well aware that sexuality is a tool to achieve or lose social status. The establishment of social rank and the acquisition of power were crucial activities in the lives of teens and, unfortunately, there appeared to be gendered winners and losers in this work. Moreover, while boys and girls eschewed the dangers of sexual encounters with strangers, the flip is positioned dangerously on the boundaries between insider and outsider.

WHO WILL GUIDE BOYS?

Parents

While there were some exceptions to the rule, most boys were reluctant and some even expressed disdain for the notion of talking to their parents about sexting. Parents may have asked them about the topic, but teens were careful to preserve their privacy, using their own brand of logic to defend their position.

> Alvin: Right. Well, like, and personal life experience, an example is I just got the picture out of nowhere. And my mom is like—she's always been like, "You can talk to me about anything." But to me, there was nothing to talk about, since I didn't ask for it and I didn't know about. It just kind of came. So like I don't really talk to anybody about anything, really, like to adults. I just keep it to myself and the closest people to me, just friends. (Ohio: Norse)

That said, boys were strongly aware of the concerns parents would have regarding behavior such as sexting, including the high expectations their parents hold for their behavior, parents' fears young people will have early sex, the differing values parents may hold from teens, and parents' concern for the effects that acts such as sexting could have on other members in the family.

> Frederick: [I]t might cause a problem for the household, I guess it depends on … his parents, then. If they were old school parents, like you're supposed to court a girl, you know, meet her parents first. Like sex wouldn't even like probably be on your mind, like that. Because you knew how to do things. And there was a certain way. And then, once you got married and—It all depends on how your parents were also raised too. (Ohio: Norse)

Some youth were not sure their parents would even know to be worried about sexting:

> Finn: I don't think they do either [talk to parents about sexting], because most parents don't even know how to text, or they'll be like, "What is sexting?" They're—some might not even know that you can actually send pictures. (Massachusetts: Gateway City)

Other Adults

Boys painted a bleak picture of educators' abilities to address gender, sexuality, adolescent development, and the many issues related to these topics. Their critique took two forms: 1) reporting on what they have experienced and describing how they imagine an adult would react to the issue, and 2) describing the cultural norms restricting communication with school adults and other adults in the community.

While boys reported they have had some sex education in school, they also remarked that it seldom covered topics like sexting. Another place where sexting might arise is in a decision-making class. In the following complex quote, boys from Massachusetts described their encounter with sexting in such a class.

> Frank: We did a lot. I mean, I didn't pay attention to half of it, being completely honest. But it was more of—I felt that our teacher was just preaching his opinions and saying that was the right way, and so it was kind of like the typical "don't get a person pregnant, you can prevent it, STDs [Sexually Transmitted Diseases] can be prevented." They didn't really touch that much on sexting, other than our teacher kind of—uh, he kind of complained about it.
>
> Grey: We had, like, three units. One was drugs, one was personal health, and then the other one was sex. And that was like the last thing we covered. We had half of the amount of time to cover it, because we had a different course also. Like, it was an advisory course on one day, and then we'd have Decisions, and then advisory the next day, and then Decisions. And so the curriculum already was cut in half, and so we had barely any time to talk about sex at all. And the teacher really didn't know what he was saying. I think he's ...
>
> Interviewer: So did he just mention sexting in passing? Was that how it was?
>
> Frank: Well, he—it felt like he pulled something out of the 1990s, like, one of those outdated videos ... He did, like, an IM [Instant Messaging] thing over the Internet, which was from, like— probably before I was even born. And it was, like, kids—you could tell because the kids dressed differently, the computers were gray and, like, that wide. Like—and it was more of a chat room thing, and it wasn't really relating at all. And that was one of the only videos we watched on the sexting unit, which we had, like, a week on, total class time. (Massachusetts: Romney)

This passage describes many of the issues boys found problematic with school coverage of issues like sex and/or sexting, including outdated materials, opinionated teachers with pat answers, poor curriculum planning leading to truncated coverage of key issues, faculty without technological knowledge adequate to understand the topic, and, what is implied although not actually said, an instructor with little liking or respect for teen opinions or authentic participation.

Boys feared speaking to those in school because they believed adults would 'chew them out,' they would face punishment, or counselors might tell their parents. They also worried adults would look down on them.

> Ben: ... because with a teacher, whatever ... even though they're not supposed to, you could get like ... that teacher could have this thought of that kid, like, "Oh, my God, that kid's like a slut" or something, because they did this. And then that teacher could look down on that person and it could be noticeable to that person and make them feel even worse. (Ohio: Norse)

It is interesting to note that this quote is unusual for the use of slut as a form of non-gendered term, applying to boys as well as girls.

Some boys in our study reported that teachers had been warned not to talk about sexting with youth. They were aware that teachers could get themselves in trouble by raising the subject with youth.

Finally, there is the issue of culture. Boys indicated they subscribe to a youth culture that enforces silence toward adults. As Abraham in the Make-Up group in South Carolina reported, if caught, boys will not tell adults anything because they do not want to be labelled a snitch or a tattletale.

Despite boys' overall negative assessment of relationships with educators, some boys were able to identify islands of connection within the larger sea of disconnection they encountered in school. These connections were made with teachers and coaches who had the capacity for rapport with young adults.

> Clayton: I feel like it depends on the teacher. If you have like—let's say a coach is, you know, a teacher too—and you spend probably more hours with the coach or with that teacher than you do at home, I feel like you open up to them more than your parents will. But you're at school a lot. So that's—Like we play football. We don't get out to like 8: 00, maybe real late. So that depends on your relationship with a person there, the teacher.
>
> Frederick: I also agree with Clayton—when he said it depends on the teacher. Because like I have a teacher-slash-coach like who I

> could talk to about anything. And he would like share his experiences too. Like I look at him as a big brother. Because I really didn't have like a father figure. So whenever I need like a male figure, I can go to him about it. And we've just got that good bond. (Ohio: Norse)

While many boys reported there were few school adults to connect to about these issues, boys' greater participation in athletics and the presence of athletic coaches in their lives may actually provide them with more options for adult connection in a high school or community setting than is afforded to girls in the same locations.

Interestingly, boys in Ohio appeared to have more positive things to say about connections to adults in schools than did youth at the other sites where the study was conducted.

BOYS' LIVES IN THESE CHANGING TIMES

Boys viewed sexting as a form of sex, acknowledging it as one of the many ways they expressed their sexuality. At the same time, they shied away from using the term sexting, focusing more on the actual practice in which they were engaged, such as forwarding or receiving.

Analysis of this data suggests teen boys were empowered in sexual arenas, with fewer inhibitions than girls, and were able to express their sexual desire more directly.

In their competitive drive for social power and ranking within peer groups, boys used their sexuality and the acquisition of sexual favors from girls (such as photos).

Boys recognized there is a clearly identified double standard in regard to how boys who engage in sexting are viewed versus girls who engage in sexting. Boys who engage in sexting do not face the shame of terms like slut and whore, as they are applied to girls. Indeed, boys' actions may be tolerated, shrugged off, or even praised, at least by peers.

While there was great pressure for boys to prove themselves sexually, to take the lead, and demonstrate their sexual prowess, doing so put them in danger from the wrath of parents, school rules, and severe penalties from legal institutions. Unfortunately, most appeared to lack appropriate knowledge about the legal penalties they could incur.

In the discussion of the flip, we have evidence that within youth culture boys can be perpetrators of a kind of social class degradation through sexuality creating a class of marginal women who are identified as 'for sexual use only.' Once identified as such, both boys and girls enforce the terms that keep these females in this position. Girls who are labelled as flips are considered highly promiscuous, existing on the border between non-paid and paid sex. Boys who are highly promiscuous do not have a label or positioning similar to that described by the term flip.

Boys were not deaf to the messages of parents or other adults regarding the potential dangers of sexting. They heard, but often followed the logic of their peer culture, which eschews discussions of sexuality with adults.

Sadly, boys described a school world in which the topics that are of most concern to them—sex and relationships—were poorly addressed. Ironically, while boys offered criticism of the ways schools address these issues, boys, through their participation in athletics and their sustained interaction with coaches whom they like and admire, may actually have access to more adult resources than girls.

COMPARING THE VIEWS OF GIRLS AND BOYS

Sexting is a term imposed on young people from the outside. From an insider's perspective, youth describe sexting as a range of practices in which intimate relationships, desire, and sexuality are expressed. Just as with sex, sexting (sexual selfies or texts with sexual expressions) serves many purposes in the pursuit of engagement with a person of interest, and our participants described many kinds of motivations and scenarios in which sexually oriented texts or photos might be exchanged one-to-one, or, in less fortunate episodes, broadcast widely.

Modern digital technology is a means by which the personal aims of intimacy may be achieved, but youth are loath to equate technology itself with the notion of sex. As they point out, many kinds of technologies have been used over the ages to assist in the furthering of romance and/or sexual engagement, from handwritten letters to the Kodak instamatic camera.

There is interesting evidence here of the ways courtship and romance may be changing in the digital world. New etiquette is emerging. For instance, when you break up with someone you should erase all the photos of the relationship from your phone. A young man pointed out that it is always a good thing to ask a girl ahead of time if she is comfortable with sexting and don't assume everyone is. In a similar vein, youth assume their phones will be shared. They pass them back and forth among acquaintances, allowing friends to view the various artifacts collected there. These are only a few of the many new standards that are present in relationships in the digital age.

Both girls and boys appear to be in agreement in regard to the ambiguity of what sexting means and the important role of digital technology in modern romance. Significant differences between girls and boys arise as we delve more deeply into the material on motivations and perspectives; here is where entrenched gendered differences in society begin to emerge.

Also, both girls and boys perceive the most prominent motivations for sexting to be the search for intimate, trusting relationship with another human being, concerns about social control and the exercise of power within the peer group, and the desire for sex. All three elements are part of both gendered perspectives, but girls and boys place different priorities on these concerns.

Girls emphasize romance and intimate one-on-one relationships as the major motivation for being drawn into a sexting scenario. Girls also recognize the power the peer group and social environment exercises in the context of developing intimate relationships and how it, too, influences a young person's decision to engage in sexting. They are aware that competition for a variety of social goods takes place in the context of sexual pursuit—from the conquest of older males and elevation of status through connection with popular boys, to gaining attention from rivals and vanquishing one's social enemies. While sexuality is clearly an important thread woven through the fabric of romance, girls tend not to allude directly to sexual desire. In girls' conversations, sexuality is submerged within romance.

Boys, on the other hand, are direct and clear about their interest in sex. Sexual desire is prominently represented in their conversation. They are also quick to describe the ways sexting supports boy's social and peer goals through serving as a venue for competition with other males. Male competition spans many areas of boys' concern from affirmation regarding personal appearance, attractiveness, and sexual maturity, to a demonstration of their ability to gain the attention, attachment, and conquest of females. Participating in this competition is crucial to the ways males rank each other within the peer group and are ranked by females within their circle of acquaintances. Given this, it was surprising to learn that boys are also, at times, surprisingly romantic.

It is important to note the similarities and differences in the ways girls and boys compete for social goods through engagement in sexting. Girls seek attention from a particular boy, affirmation of their overall attractiveness, and confirmation of their social stature. Boys often engage in sexting to brag and swagger, as they and girls describe it. They use relationships with girls as another venue for male competition. Many boys express considerable concern about the size of their sexual apparatus in comparison to other males.

Both girls and boys argue vigorously for a notion of inherency in regard to female and male characteristics. For instance, girls are seen to be more vulnerable, needing of protection, and, in the face of criticism or exposure for sexual activities, even in danger (in the worst case scenario) of committing suicide. Boys, on the other hand, are seen as not particularly caring about critique for their sexual activities, and as less vulnerable to the slings and arrows of criticism. While they are expected to protect girls, they are also expected to pursue them.

In the sexual game between the two genders, girls are pursued and boys are pursuing. Girls flirt and boys try to break down the gates. Girls need protection, and parents and other adults are more likely to provide such protection to them than to boys whom they think are less vulnerable. Girls, however, are also desirous (although they indicate their feelings are more romantic), and are complicit with boys in working around the barriers placed between them by adults.

Not surprisingly, our participants also describe significant differences in the consequences females and males face when they engage in sexting. Girls who engage in sexting and are publicly exposed face shaming from their peers and application of the labels of slut, whore, flip, bus (yes, we heard that one too), and probably other terms as well. This reaction sounds much like what Nathaniel Hawthorne's Hester Prynne endured in *The Scarlet Letter*, and, indeed, the reaction may spring from similar wellsprings of our culture.

While boys may describe themselves in passing as a slut or whore, the terms are borrowed and do not stick in the same way as they do to girls. A boy who is easy or promiscuous does not face the same shaming as a girl, and may gain status through his conquests and the trophies he collects in the form of photographs of girls.

As mentioned earlier, shaming of girls goes beyond the circle of peers (female and male), stretching out to family (parents and siblings), extended family (aunts, uncles, grandparents), and beyond. A girl can bring great shame on her family, and the girl and her family may be shunned by friends and neighbors.

The example of the flip raised uncomfortable questions for which there are no easy answers. A flip is a young girl who is seasoned by men to assume a role in society that is ambivalently close to paid sex work. The term was introduced by participants of South Carolina's African-American culture, and yet there are undoubtedly parallel terms and positioning that occurs across our society. Both girls and boys in South Carolina locations were aware of the term and agreed to its meaning. The flip is an unsolved issue that I will return to at the conclusion of this book.

Within families, from youth perspectives mothers are assumed to play a key role in educating and monitoring teen sexual behavior. Fathers, it appears, are important in terms of discipline. In particular, fathers are considered important in protecting girls from the pressures brought to bear by boys. Boys worry about the wrath of fathers who are protecting a female child.

While the law is assumed to be applied equally to girls and boys, there is a sense from the transcripts that boys may be more vulnerable to the current laws or seen to be so. Discussions of sex offenders and child pornographers were often accompanied by the male pronoun, not the female pronoun, indicating this may be the way it is viewed by young people. The interest older boys have in younger girls and vice versa, which both genders attest to, places more boys in the position of being overage and in relationship with girls who are underage. Thus, boys are more likely to be vulnerable to legal complaints in this area of boy/girl relationships.

Both genders feel there are significant barriers talking to parents or other adults about these issues. Within the home circle, mothers are probably the first person a teen would turn to, but many teens would prefer to keep these sexual issues to themselves.

Girls and boys generally describe adults in schools as not interested, trustworthy, or available to talk to them about these issues. The examples supporting this statement outweigh those made in defense of connection to schools. Shaming also extends to school, and girls, in particular, may be vulnerable to being shamed by adults in their schools. Interestingly, girls and boys in Ohio seemed overall more at ease with and trusting of adults in their schools than did youth in the other two locations.

Boys, however, because of their greater participation in sports and consequently their relationships with coaches, may have more access to adults they respect and will talk with than girls. It was discouraging to learn girls did not have similar adults available to them through school or community activities.

The comfort divide in technology use that exists between teens and adults in general is pointed to as a cause for some of the tension around the issue of sexting. Teens suggest adults born within the modern digital era or close to it will be most likely to share similar views with teens in regard to technology and sexuality.

An important thread weaving throughout the conversations of both boys and girls was the issue of the media and our sexualized society. Indeed, the media may feel like a third kind of adult influence in teens' lives—parents and family members, educators and community members, and the media. The adults who inform youth from the media are in many roles: newscasters and talk show hosts and celebrities of many sorts. From news, commercials, tweets, movies, and music videos, messages in the form of voices and images are broadcast to young people who absorb, integrate, and reflect parts back. These messages carry powerful content about gender, sexuality, and the ways intimate relationships should be constructed in our society.

Sexting has proven to be a powerful lens through which to understand the gendered assumptions of our society and the ways we apply these assumptions to teen girls and boys. In our society, high school-age youth have many opportunities and, as this study indicates, some alarming challenges to face as well. What are the roots of the gendered assumptions with which we endow youth? What value did these assumptions once confer, and what are the current dangers these beliefs pose to young people? What are the costs we pay for maintaining these restrictions? These are some of the questions I am left with after reviewing the many words of girls and boys talking about sexuality in their lives. They are questions I continue to ponder as I move forward into thinking about the words of adults who are concerned about youth—parents, educators, and community members.

ADULT VOICES

Section II of the book shifts attention away from the voices of youth to those adults who are most concerned and connected with youth lives.

The first chapter of Section II allows you to listen to the perspectives of teens' parents and caregivers. These individuals live day-to-day in the presence of youth and are intimately aware of the hopes, cares, fears, and challenges young people face.

The second chapter in this section provides an opportunity to hear from the many other adults present in youth lives. Many of these youth workers are in schools as teachers, counselors, nurses, and administrators. Others work in communities for community agencies, local police, health organizations, or juvenile justice programs, to name just a few of the places in which youth-centric adults can be found.

Their sentiments bear many similarities to youth, but there are also great differences in their positions, roles, content, and concerns. As with the chapters about youth, I present them in as direct and authentic a way as I can, allowing each group to speak for itself before comparing them with each other and youth.

PARENTING TEENS IN THESE DIGITAL TIMES

Parents and other primary caregivers are vital to young people's understanding of sexuality, intimacy, and gender. They are the people who held, touched, kissed, and cuddled the young ones, providing them with the earliest understanding of human intimacy and relationship. They clothed, spoke to, fed, housed, and offered education, and in each of these acts they provided information—implicit or explicit—about the meaning of gender. While each young person may have an innate, biological sense of gender, there is also a wide world of cultural and symbolic knowledge about gender that is passed on to them, and parents or caregivers in every society have been central to this work.

In asking parents to come together and speak of their views about teen sexting, we also provided parents with a significant forum in which to present their beliefs about gender, sexuality, and teens. It is truly impossible to talk about the modern phenomenon of sexting without thinking about the contexts in which today's families are operating, and the focus group discussions raised important points in regard to parental assumptions about gender and sexuality. In considering motivations for teen sexting, parents brought us deeply into their perceptions of teens and gendered behavior. Their assumptions about sexting motivations and gender had strong ties to their beliefs about the consequences females and males would face from engaging in these acts. Parents recognized their responsibility for guiding teens through these muddy waters, and at the same time they recognized that they cannot do it alone and looked outward to others who could give assistance.

GENDER IN THE CONTEXT OF SEXTING: PARENTS' DEFINITIONS AND BELIEFS OF TEEN SEXTING PRACTICES

Parents' understanding of sexting covered a wide gamut of knowledge and experience, from did not know, heard about it at church, or saw a movie about it on TV, to knew about an incident at school, heard about a suicide related to sexting, or had a child involved in online sexual activities. Discussion of what parents knew about sexting and how they first learned about it provoked many associated terms, including nude, partially clothed, underwear, inappropriate, naughty, provocative, suggestive, dirty, disgusting, unbelievable, not acceptable, pornography, exploitation, improper, exposing, compromising, and lewd. One parent referred to sexting as "a giant game of playing doctor" (Ohio: Native). Another spoke of it as "whatever arouses you" (South Carolina: Brad). The discussions of sexting raised few positive associations in the minds of the caregivers with whom we spoke.

Discussions of sexting also brought forward parents' memories of the ways sexuality and technology had been used in their pasts. These reminiscences included beepers (numbers stood for sexual acts), butts on Xerox machines (taking a photocopy of your nude bottom to share with others), the telephone party line (listening in to the conversations of young or older couples), the male locker room (sharing photographs of females), and many other interesting descriptions of the ways sexuality has been furthered by technology in different eras.

As in the teen focus groups, discussions of sexting raised the question of what is sex. Some parents believed teens did not consider sexting as real sex, and saw a parallel between teens' views of sexting and their views of oral sex (also considered by some not to be sex). They also discussed the ways sexting, if defined as not sex, could be seen as a way to have a sexual experience but preserve one's virginity.

> Ms. Ivey: I believe personally they think it's still a way of keeping their virginity. Because if they're not technically doing it, they don't have any of the consequences. I mean these teenagers have gotten, or kids have gotten smart. You know, they don't want to have babies, they don't want the STDs but hey, let's just talk about it, it's nothing wrong with talking about it. But you know, I just believe that that's one reason why. And they feel like it's no harm in just doing that. (South Carolina: Norton)

As Ms. Ivey pointed out, preserving one's virginity does not just have moral value, but is also a means of preventing pregnancy and disease. These are goals that have relevance to both girls and boys.

Interestingly, whether they liked it or not, the majority of parents and caregivers were of the opinion that sexting was probably fairly common among adolescents.

CONTEXTS OF TODAY'S FAMILIES AND THE ISSUES IMPINGING ON GENDER

Discussion of teens and sexuality takes place against a backdrop of adult concerns about our rapidly changing society, its norms, values, and practices. As parents consider what is accepted today, they compare it to what was appropriate at an earlier time and fret about what will be in the future.

Overall parents expressed significant concern about what can only be termed the breakdown of the family. When they reflected on why issues like sexting arise they pointed to:

Mrs. Bishop: I don't think these children are getting the affection and getting the security that they need at home. (Wes, South Carolina)

Mr. Isaacsen: I do think there's just been a deterioration of values and standards. And I think in our day, there was right and there was wrong, and we kind of knew the difference. And the more some of these kids are doing things, I think it's true, they just don't think twice about it. They don't know what's inappropriate and what's not. There's just no framework or no guideline for them. You know, the things I hear kids say, I mean, the language and things that they say, in my day, oh no, I said that in front of an adult. And now, these things come out of their mouths, and they just don't even know that there's anything wrong with it. (Ohio: Norse)

Two issues that figured prominently in caregiver's concerns about deteriorating standards in society were changes in technology, and the sexualized nature of society.

Technology

Parents' concerns about technology included a general orientation to technology—"it is like technology is taking over the world" (South Carolina: Brad)—to concerns about the linkage of technology and sexuality. For instance, technology makes it extremely easy for children to get to hard core pornography. Parents worried about their ability to keep up with the technological skills and knowledge of their children. Lacking these skills, they wondered if they will be able to ward off the dangers their children face in the online world.

Parents also pointed out the ways small changes in technology became large changes in social interaction. For instance, "the phone is untethered from the wall" (Ohio: Astro), meaning that telephone conversations can take place anywhere, not just in the central area of the home where all members can hear. Moreover, when texting entered the picture, the parties need no longer speak aloud. Thus, young people can hold a heated but silent conversation with peers under the noses of their parents who cannot hear the discussion.

The Sexualized Nature of Society

Caregivers were highly concerned about what they see as the sexualized nature of society and provided many examples of what they meant by this notion.

They see these changes as closely tied to changes in society's overall values about sex ("sex is no big deal to kids now days") as well as changes in the ways courtship has changed: "much more cut to the chase" (Ohio: Norse). Sexual suggestiveness raised concerns for parents as they struggled to make sense of teen behavior.

> Ms. Lamont: I guess I don't clearly understand the definition of sexting, if it's just like nudity, or very explicit language in text messages, or can it just be something that's very suggestive. There was a picture of a girl out there that we know, and she was just bent over with a pair of sweatpants on that had a hole, and there was another young lady with her finger in the hole of the sweatpants. Now I don't know if that's considered sexting. I thought it was very, very suggestive. Yeah if another person looked at it, they might go oh she's got a hole in her pants. I guess, I thought it was inappropriate, but the kids I think would think, oh that's funny, you know. I guess to me, there's maybe a generational gap between what I would consider sexting, or inappropriate, and what the kids consider inappropriate, so. (Ohio: Astro)

Parents' comments about the issue of the sexualized nature of society, while directed at teens and society overall, focused much more on concerns about girls and changes in the ways girls dress or act. They complained about the sexual nature of clothing for young girls, the uniforms of cheerleaders, and the way girls portray themselves on Facebook (the kissy face on Facebook pages of girls—Massachusetts: Gateway City). In all, comments about girls predominated in the discussion about the sexualized nature of society and its effects.

PARENTS' GENDERED UNDERSTANDINGS OF THE MOTIVATIONS FOR TEEN SEXTING

Of the three concerns used as bins for collecting teens' views regarding motivations for sexting—romance or intimacy, peers and social competition, and sex—parents were most concerned about peers and social competition as a place where youth problems could arise. They acknowledged issues of sexuality, and they had the least interest in or concern about romance or intimacy. As adults, their definitions and perspectives of these categories were unique to their stance.

Romance and Intimacy

> Mr. Carlisle: I think it's maybe romantic, it's a form of communication that has been desensitized ... I know that it's used to start a relationship. I think it's just a communication with —I don't know I have a hard time thinking of a middle school aged child as romantic, but ... (Massachusetts, Romney)

This quotation from Mr. Carlisle spoke with strength to caregivers' perspectives on romance and teens. They acknowledged the term, but doubted its veracity when applied to the activities of young people. While they discussed girls' interest, in particular, in finding that certain someone and expressing 'I love you,' these activities were not given serious respect. Teens were considered people with quickly changing moods and interests, and the suggestion was that their romantic interests are not to be taken too seriously. It may also be true that romance, with the implication of mutual trust, is a positive thing by its very nature and did not warrant the level of concern that other motivations provoked for adults.

Peers and Social Competition

Parents had strong concerns about the dangers arising when sexting accompanies the drive for social status, competition, and control. From their experience, this is where the most damage occurs. They believed teens' desire to achieve among their peers could lead them to take risks and act in ways that may be satisfying in the immediate present but could bring them harm in the future.

Parents spoke of the importance of the in-crowd, the desire for approval, and the need to fit in and find their place.

> Ms. Erikson: I think some of it is attention, especially teenage years that you need approval of peers, and social groups are so much more important than their approval necessarily of their parents, or people of our generation ... and I think [some teens] are saying, you know, like say something outlandish, and I get a hundred people saying they like it on Facebook. This is positive attention, I'm popular, and I think that's a very important thing for them at that age. (Ohio: Astro)

As Ms. Erikson pointed out, the online world itself has created new mechanisms for judging peer approval: the liking of an item. Because the number of likes is recorded and visible to all who view an item, high numbers of likes become an incentive to search for more ways to gain peer approval.

In discussing the issue of peer approval, adults, like teens, turned toward the notion of humor or joking. Adults recognized the notion of the joke as a double-edged sword, a comment that is ambivalent, capable of being positive or negative at the same time.

> Ms. Franklin: So I think it is a form of, you know, bullying, humiliation. I think they think it's a joke, they think it's funny, but the thing of it is, you can't take it back. (Massachusetts: Andrews)

Adults were also aware that photographs themselves can become the joke through mischievous changes made possible by technological wizardry. Ms. Garland described how this same effect was achieved in a pre-digital era, but then went on to discuss how the understanding of a communication changes shape as it moves into different settings. Parents like Ms. Garland worried that messages today can be seen by anyone in any part of the world, and what was once a peer-related incident becomes a much wider concern.

> Ms. Garland: I remember ... they put a different body on one of my friend's face. And it was like a joke, and it was really a joke, but that was out there then. And so that could go around to everybody. It was like, it was a joke. And I've talked to my kids a lot about that, that you can't tell those things if it's a joke. I've talked to them a lot about texting, that you can't read tone. So I might say, oh my god, I hate—yeah, you know, I'm joking with you, I hate you, kiddingly. Now you've read it as she hates me.

So then you're telling her, you know, oh my god, did you know so and so hates me? And all of a sudden, that joke has blown up, and into something. And that's one of the big lessons I've talked to the kids about. Saying, what you put out there to one person can go to everybody in the world, and the way you say things can be quickly changed because no one really knows how you're saying it. (Massachusetts: Andrews)

Sex

Caregivers were well aware of teens' changing bodies and maturing sexual capacities.

> Mr. Dumont: I think that it's also the manifestation of just they're growing and becoming sexual people, you know? They have hormones, and technology, and you know, unfortunately pornography, and a lot of—and a world that's pretty sensualized around them. And lots of bad examples. (Massachusetts: Romney)

Mr. Dumont added together the dangers of this maturing sexuality in a way that expressed the concerns of many parents: sexuality + technology + sexualized society = trouble.

Ms. Hood tied the issue of sex back to concerns about social competition, raising a baseball metaphor that has long been used to discuss the comparison of achieving sexual favors by men—getting to the bases.

> Ms. Hood: I think the difference is, the same thing for men, because they just been like the centers, I think that men do it to see how far they can get. You know, when we was younger, it was bases, first base, second, whatever. Now they're just trying to figure out far they can go, and how far the girl is going to let them go … So, even with the guy, I think it's still always with the guy, it's just how far I can go, and with girls, it's I've done more than you did, or I done more than you did. (South Carolina: Brad)

Embedded in this example is the notion that male sexuality is still the same as it was in some earlier time, but that female sexuality has changed and now incorporates new and more aggressive elements.

Girls: Have They Changed?

By far and away, parents illustrated their concerns about teens and sexuality with examples related to girls' behaviors. Moreover, their examples overwhelmingly portrayed girls' changed sexual behavior in a negative light. Many of their comments were direct and critical.

> Ms. Lamont: It used to be that the boys were kind of potty mouths, and the girls always needed to appear prim and proper. Now, what I've seen on Facebook, the girls could make some of these guys blush. Certainly do me. I mean I am just amazed at some of the vulgarity, just on Facebook, and just statements that are made for absolutely no reason, not in a conversation, just a little log-in, and type just a phrase, and I'm thinking, where is your mother? How come your mother hasn't washed your mind out with soap, because they'll just say things, and so I don't know that there's a difference there anymore. I mean the guys can certainly, you know, say, but I think you always expected, no offense, but the boys expected more out of—more of that kind of stuff out of guys than girls, but the girls are right there with them now, and I see it every day because I go on Facebook every day, and I'm probably going to regret saying this, but I have—I have an alter-ego, that I [use to] log into Facebook, and it's amazing that these kids will friend somebody that they've never heard of in their life, and the things that you can see, just appalling and unbelievable. (Ohio: Astro)

Many adults, like Ms. Lamont, were concerned about the changing norms in daily language, particularly the increase in swearing and sexual content. Indeed for many in our focus groups, changes in technology were synonymous with the increased sexual nature of society and changing language norms, and these changes were seen to be affecting girls in particularly negative ways.

Other comments described what they perceived to be girls' essential nature. Their depictions, while framed as objective, overall placed girls in a more negative light and boys in a more benign light. Girls were seen as more aggressive now, as more revengeful (than boys), concerned with keeping up with their friends, throwing themselves at boys, and teasing and flirting with boys. In the focus groups, speakers commented that girls mature earlier than boys, they want to appear older than they are, and they are trying to prove they are really women. These kinds of comments about girls were offered by focus group participants across many lines of questioning.

Indeed in one passage, inappropriate sexual behavior was described as part of a multi-generational female heritage.

> Ms. Gardner: You know how they talk about, you've got to break the chain? Sometimes it's been in their family. It's what their grandmother did, it's what their mother did, and now it's what they're doing and you just—it's like some people don't ever break that cycle … I can think of an instance where you can go back and be the great-grandmother, the grandmother did it, the mother did it, and now the child is doing it.
>
> Ms. Avery: In other words a family tradition.
>
> Ms. Gardner: You don't ever break that cycle, so it just is what you've learned. (South Carolina: Wes)

There was no such parallel description of male heritage issues anywhere in the data collected.

TEEN SEXTING: PARENTAL VIEWS OF THE GENDERED CONSEQUENCES

Like teens, in discussing consequences parents juggled the dual notions of personal and legal consequences. In their responses there was more elaboration about personal consequences than there was about legal consequences. They were aware of the existence of legal consequences, but often had vague and inconclusive ideas of what these were. Of great concern to parents (as it was to teens) was whether or not the legal consequence took into account the context and motivations of the teens involved.

> Ms. Kennedy: We had discussed it before at my house, because I saw it on television before it even happened in this general area. The thing I think is kind of disturbing is, once again, it's between kids who are kind of stupid and impulsive, and then they get charged with being sexual predators. They're getting put in jail. I get it's a stupid mistake, but I'm also like, that's a little extreme, I think, in my book. There has to be some kind of middle ground for that, because it's just some kid did something stupid. (Ohio: Astro)

Parents' personal concerns in regard to sexting were balanced between the present and the future. In the present they feared their children could be psychologically hurt (embarrassed, humiliated, or bullied) and that this could lead to debilitating results. They recognized how dangerous it can be to be labelled, lose friends, or suffer loss of reputation or social status. They recognized that there may be a number of intermediate reactions to these hurts, but that suicide could be the ultimate conclusion to deep hurts.

As with youth, parents mentioned girls in regard to suicide, but no boy examples were given. In the following passage, Ms. Burke mentioned girls and suicide twice in responding to questioning about legal consequences. The male example she gave is football superstar Brett Favre who was publicly exposed for sexting, but who to the best of my knowledge did not express serious psychological concerns about his act. Indeed, here, as with youth, suicide seemed to be a girl default position.

> Ms. Burke: I think the best way we can look forward to helping this is the way we teach a lot of things in the school system, is to show them that extreme examples and what has happened to the consequences. So the one girl who committed suicide because of her friends—well, maybe not her friends—but them being vicious, you know, through the sexting kinds of messages. Kids learn through seeing consequences, you know, visually, and talking about them. And I think that should be part of the education system, not just at home. But yet the media is already doing it. Because whenever we see a harmful consequence of someone through sexting, you know, whether it's Brett Favre or high school girls that have committed suicide because of not being able to cope with what they viewed as a malicious gang-up attack on them. (Ohio: Native)

When caregivers looked into the future, they worried about the impact the revelation of a sexting incident could have on college, military applications, and employment.

Future concerns also included the notion of documentation that will never go away—an indecent photo or impetuous text that others will always be able to find and connect to their child so that, despite the passage of time, that one indiscrete moment continues to live on in virtual space.

> Ms. Anthony: Where it was a bullying situation, her picture wound up on the web, and the parent did everything they could to get it down, but because it's in cyberspace, it stays there forever, it's now being sold in China as child porn, and she never intended it to be out there. (Massachusetts: Andrews)

Passages such as the one above that discuss the everlasting effects of the Internet often have the eerie sense of urban legends, regardless of the truth of what is reported.

In this complex passage provided by Ms. Hood in South Carolina (Brad), the legal and personal consequences were intricately knitted together with concerns about sexuality and developmental maturity.

> Ms. Hood: I think that if we put more into the mind—I think because teens do a lot of things that we think makes them mature, I think put a lot on them that we think they should know, and they really don't know, and I think just like bullying, and the different levels of that, sexting is the same way, they have different levels of that, and I think that a lot of things that we think they know about, like bullying is not something that's legal. Harassment is not legal. Sexual harassment is worse. So you would think that a teenage child would understand that there are consequences to this, but most girls don't even understand that you ain't ready for sex, until you're at least 21. So their mind does not mature, because once you get that, you can't take it back. So a lot of things that we think the kids understand, especially about laws, and the wrongness of whatever, a lot of teens don't understand and you'd think they would, but they don't. They don't. Just like they don't understand the consequences. All they know is, if I have sex, I'll get pregnant, but they don't understand that once I have sex with this person, and he don't like me again in the morning, that's going to hurt me worse than getting pregnant. You see what I'm saying? So it's the mature level of the child, they're still children to me. It's the mature level of the child. It's how much the parents are communicating with the child ... and just because they tell you that they understand stuff, it does not mean that they understand. That's my point. They don't know as much as we think they know.

As this mother recognized, the legal and the personal are always linked in complicated fashion, and she was well aware of the experience it takes to make sense of intimacy, desire, and relationship. Speaking as mother to daughter and then to all youth, she looked at the situation with the perspective that comes from having lived and experienced both good and bad choices. This is the wisdom that leaves parents shuddering for the young.

FROM PARENTS' PERSPECTIVES: WHO WILL GUIDE TEENS?

Caregivers instruct their wards daily. They create policies and directives, model and give examples. With the words and examples they use to shepherd young people's sexuality, they invariably are also giving voice to their notions of gender and acceptable gendered behavior. These instructions are embedded within the home setting and also include the presence and behavior of other adults and young people. Parents' policies and perspectives can be both enduring (values that stand the test of time) and mutable (views that are changed with circumstances and new experience).

> Ms. Collins: Well I think about pornography. I think about exploitation when you talk about sexting. My son told me about sexting. He educated me and we talked. I think that the remedy to a lot of things is trying to educate your kids and give them values. And if you give them those values in the beginning, they then know what's acceptable behavior and what's not. And I know we have peer pressure, but still they know right and wrong. There are some things they may do. They may use language that may be inappropriate, and I don't like that, but if I had a preference, I'd rather a teeny bit of that than thinking about the sexting kind of thing going on. (South Carolina: Wes)

Ms. Collins described how new practices such as sexting or swearing brought about new family policies and outlooks. In the situation she discussed, she assisted her son in interpreting social developments using the values she hoped to inculcate in him.

Parents discussed their concerns about boys and girls. There were, however, special concerns expressed about girls' vulnerability and the changing norms of society.

> Ms. Emerson: Okay, and you know what? I am a—I won't say [I am] a Sally do-gooder at heart, but my whole belief behind that kind of stuff is we as parents teach our daughters that they have to have respect in themselves, that doing that kind of thing, they're not doing anything for them. The only person who is really going to get any pleasure out of it is the person of the opposite sex. They're not going to think about them twice. You know, be up front, talk about it, discuss it, but teach your child to respect herself more than that, way more than that. Personal opinion.
>
> Ms. Flynn: I think that just the whole term dating has changed. So when we were growing up, you went out on a date and the boy

came and got you in his clunker, and you went out, he paid, he brought you home and that was it. I don't know—my daughter has never been on a date, she's 17. I don't know if this sexting is part of … dating—I don't know. (South Carolina: Wes)

In terms of guidance for young people, women offered a unique example of how they stayed on top of problems and monitored behavior through what I would refer to as the moms club. There was no such example presented by men of the use of a group to share information about teen behavior in order to head off problems.

Ms. Inez: … I have daughters in high school, so I have a junior and I have a freshman, and we have a lot of kids that come around. It's actually amazing—you guys would really be shocked at how many people and how many kids are doing this. These kids are very readily talking about it. It's amazing, and the only thing that I can say, as parents, you've got to talk to each other. Because when one of the kids said, "Oh, I did this," or whatever the case may be, these kids are just clearly talking about it. I'm immediately on the phone with my friends, saying, "Yeah, you need to stop this now." We as parents actually talk without the kids knowing. Because if they know that we're talking, then they won't open up. So we actually back door, literally, to each other, very secretively. I hate to say that, but we really do. We'll meet somewhere for lunch or whatever, and we all literally catch up on what's happening. The moms kind of collectively know what's going on, but I am shocked at how often this is happening in the kids. (Ohio: Astro)

Ms. Inez provided an interesting example of the ways parenting styles and options may differ significantly across genders. This was yet another wrinkle in the complex gendered puzzle of adolescence.

In regard to the notion of responsibility, a surprising finding was the significant amount of time and space parents devoted to criticism of parents as the problem variable in curbing youth involvement in sexting. Parents in this study worried about parents who seem to be abdicating, unaware of, or indifferent to the importance of their role in teaching youth values. Our participants advocated for parents to take an active role in monitoring youth behavior and their technology use.

These criticisms conveyed implicit gendered messages in regard to responsibility. For instance, earlier it was mentioned that caregivers were concerned, in particular, about the sexuality displayed in girls' clothing choices. The implied message could be that parents are not monitoring girls appropriately in this area, and thus, girls are demonstrating a lack of values knowledge.

CONCLUSION

Caregivers, as adults charged with the oversight of young people, are naturally more cautious and concerned than their younger charges. If they sound more negative, judgmental, or less buoyant than the youth described in earlier chapters, it is not surprising, as they bear the responsibility for the safety, health, and well-being of the young people. Experienced with the cares of the world, they are concerned with the many dangers that can be found in the wider world of media, malls, and school as well. They believe the best preparation they can give young people to face these challenges is grounding in values—what is right, what is wrong, how do you recognize one from the other, how do you stand up for yourself, and how do you stand up for others. These are the challenges that test character and from which character is shaped.

Today's digitalized world is significantly different than the world in which caregivers were raised. Between cell phones and the Internet, digital photos and Skype, every day is a challenge to learn the next new thing and respond to the implications it may have for their children.

While definitely more somber than youth in their discussions of sexting, parents were also quick to acknowledge the ways sex and dating before the Internet bore much in common with sex and dating in digital times. They waxed humorous over the silliness of their youth, relationships with their own parents, and the crazy things they were capable of once upon a time.

Hovering in the background, behind the generalized discussion of sexting, parents expressed enduring themes about gender that were reminiscent of what was heard from many youth.

> Ms. Inez: Don't you think it also kind of goes back to the way girls and guys essentially think at that age, though? Girls tend to be a little bit more emotional. Guys are maybe a little bit more matter-of-fact. I haven't met that many boys, with my daughters anyway, that put themselves out there. They're not rushing to go, oh, I love you. But these girls are just running to say the words. I think that, with girls, the one thing I've tried to express to all the girls that come to our house is, you have to set the pace. You set the pace, essentially, for what's going to happen in any relationship you get into. The boys are like, well, heck—they're willing to—so it's so different to hear the boys come and give

me their—in my high school, we used to say – that was a couple years ago—we used to say, "That's another notch for my bedpost." (Ohio: Astro)

In this iconic quotation, Ms. Inez put into words what we heard across the many parent focus groups: girls set the pace, boys notch the bedpost. Moreover, she expressed what seems to be a widely held belief among adults and teens, that girls want love, but boys want sex. While described in many different ways through the voices of many different parent participants, these are basic messages that are widely subscribed to in our society.

OTHER ADULTS IN YOUNG PEOPLE'S LIVES

Participants in the Other Adult category—educators, legal and safety, and community leaders—used a trifocal lens with which to view young people. Through one part of the lens they perceived youth behavior through the requirements and goals of their employer or profession. Through another part of the lens, they viewed youth in comparison to their own children, grandchildren or other youth to whom they were close when not in their professional role. Through the third part of the lens, they looked at youth with the perspective of their own youthful experiences, often a view of youth prior to the presence of the Internet. The multiple relationships those in the Other Adult category possessed toward young people illustrated the deeply embedded sense of time experienced in adult lives—who we have been, who we are, and who we will be.

In this chapter my goal is to dig deeply into the perspectives of adults who spoke from multiple professional roles in their work with youth. As educators, they served in roles as teachers, counselors, and administrators. Many worked in schools and with police and enforcement as school resource officers. District attorney's offices and juvenile court officials were also represented in our groups. Finally, a number of community organizations with strong interest in youth participated in the focus group discussions. The key question I ask here is: how are youth seen through these many professionals' eyes, and in particular, how are their gendered and sexual differences understood by those who are charged with youth safety, health, and growth when they are outside of their parents' care?

DEFINING SEXTING

Although those in the Other Adult category are exposed to information about sexting through professional development opportunities, they are no more sure of what sexting is than adults in the parental category or youth themselves. These adults struggled to describe sexting in discussions that ranged from the visual (pictures, photos, and videos) to the linguistic (spoken words or text). They considered the role of actions from forwarding and receiving to sending. Ms. Quentin from Ohio expressed the confusion felt as groups tried to define sexting:

Ms. Quentin: I think for me the obvious examples are easy to find for me—that are obvious. You know, the pictures, some of the other examples people have given. Where I fall down a little bit is appropriate versus inappropriate, you know, exactly what is that definition? Does it go down to certain words? I mean does that cover flirting and what is over the line with flirting? And so it gets a little bit confusing on those areas for me. (Ohio: Focus Group 1)

The significant thread represented here is the complexity of the practice: that is, the ways sexting is embedded in a context that includes one and often more people, in a variety of acts that can vary over time and make use of different media. The interpretation of these acts varies with the experience and values one brings to the incident, the understanding of motivations and participants, and the role one occupies when the act is encountered. For instance, teachers and administrators might view a sexting incident differently than a school resource officer or someone from the district attorney's office. The act is perceived differently when it is considered flirting as opposed to sexual predation. Interpretation of sexting acts, as Ms. Quentin's comments illustrates, is not an easy task.

MAKING SENSE OF SEXTING IN TODAY'S DIGITAL, SEXUALIZED WORLD

Ms. Lawrence: I feel 100 years old sometimes. I was born in the early '60s, so I benefited from all the various movements, whether it was civil rights, women's movement, sexual revolution, so I am by no means what I would call the prude of my parent's generation, but I'm still astounded. They say Baby Boomers have done the worst job of raising kids. I think we probably have. I'm amazed at those little shorts that the girls wear, that say like hot. What parent would allow that for [a] daughter, let alone buy them. These parents are buying these clothes, let alone allowing them to wear them, and then they're surprised when their kids have sex, and send pictures of themselves ...

... the problem with the Internet, and communication, is that we learned how to use the Internet before we learned how to use the Internet, and I think that's really the problem, and we're given this amazing technology, and we're all like, we're so good at this, we know how to use our computers, and use the Internet, but we still as a society, I don't think we really understood the

OTHER ADULTS IN YOUNG PEOPLE'S LIVES

implication, whether it's terrorists making bombs because they learned how to use the Internet, or from groups, or it's sexting, or it's predators, whatever it is, I don't think we as a society have really reined in this technology. (Massachusetts, J2, Other Adult Focus Group)

In this passage, Ms. Lawrence spoke for many in the Other Adult category. Important themes she raised are the tension around time and culture, that is, time and culture as they existed before the Internet, and time and culture as they are perceived after the advent of the Internet. The coming of the Internet into our lives is a moment that today's adults, who live with a foot in both eras, perceived as a crucial marker. As Ms. Lawrence suggested, the social upheavals of the 20th century (the civil rights movement and women's movement, for instance) may not be as momentous in her mind, or the minds of other adults with whom we spoke, as the social upheaval they feel from the presence of the Internet. With the Internet, they fear something has been unleashed that cannot be controlled, a power that may destroy us before we will be able to define and regulate it.

As is often the case in discussing sexting and technology, adults openly commented on their feelings about the sexualized nature of society, and when they did so, they turned their attention toward girls and perceptions of their sexualized behaviors. They found girls' dress and behavior to be problematic. The speaker suggested that the women's movement led to greater possibilities of choice among girls and a stronger sense of independence in regard to approaching boys, but these changes have also led, in her opinion, to more young people having sex and the rise of sexting.

Ms. Lawrence was not an anomaly; rather her comments were highly representative of the ways a range of discourses—social movements of the 60s, the implementation of the Internet, and current youth culture—were brought together by adults as a discursive whole.

Ms. McLaughlin, another educator from Massachusetts, voiced ideas similar to Ms. Lawrence when she said:

Ms. McLaughlin: … I think too, when you look back at girls, women, whatever, it used to be, that the male was the one that asked you out and you had to kind of like wait to hear—well those days are gone. And having these handheld devices make it even easier, if you're still kind of a wallflower and you don't necessarily want to go up and talk to someone to their face or ask them, whatever, you text them or you send them something or, it's another way for them to be equal. They can do the same thing they can do,

not be as intimidated or whatever. (Massachusetts, J1, Other
Adult Focus Group)

In the passages above, Ms. Lawrence criticized the sexual behavior of girls,
identifying the problem with poor parenting, and Ms. McLaughlin
criticized the sexual behavior of girls, laying the problem at the feet of
technology and changes in gendered practices in society. In both instances,
the critique was with girls, and we do not know what young men's
problems may be or how their actions are illustrative of the issue of
sexualized nature of society. Indeed, if anything, boys and men were
depicted (through their absence) as victims of the women's movement and
modern social change. They have lost their voices and capacity for action.
It is not too simplistic to state that women were depicted as acting on men,
and male views were not or could not be expressed. While I have not
shared quotations from men in this section, our analysis (admittedly based
upon a larger sampling of women than men) did not reveal a significantly
different male perception.

MOTIVATIONS FOR SEXTING AND THEIR GENDERED IMPLICATIONS

Those in the Other Adult category were overall rather negative in
discussing motivations for teen sexting. Sexting, from their perspectives,
was primarily a problem, and this viewpoint carried over to their evaluation
of why young people sext. They were reluctant to ascribe romance or
intimacy as a legitimate motivation for teen sexting. They believed that
peer issues—the search for control, legitimacy, status, etc.—were highly
significant motivations behind teen sexting incidents. They also believed
that the desire for sexual involvement or expression ranks high as a
motivation for youth. Adults also subscribed to a category of motivation
that I would call dismissive or happenstance: that is, engagement in sexting
that is accidental, experimental, or done out of boredom. Finally, not
surprisingly, adults suggested that technology itself is to blame as a
motivation for sexting.

Romance

Ms. Lake: I think it's about perception as well. What we might
perceive as not being romantic or just whatever, these two kids
might be completely just infatuated with each other and feel that

it's romantic. While we may not see it like that, they may feel that it is romantic. (Ohio, Other Adult Focus Group 1)

Adults, looking at young people with the hindsight of their own personal experience with romantic relationships, were skeptical of the depth and longevity of teen couples. As a result, they questioned whether or not teen relationships would stand the test of time and trust.

Peer Social Hierarchy—Power and Ranking

A large portion of the comments by adults on youth motivation in sexting were about the way sexting plays a role in the social hierarchy of teen life, where status and power are sought within and across peer groups and gender affiliations. Sexting as a tool for class movement was made clear in this comment:

> Mr. Stanton: I actually spoke to a student who sent a sext in photograph of his girlfriend electronically to his friends and I asked him why'd you do that. And he specifically said to me, well, right now he said, as you know, there are three levels of sociality. And I was on the bottom level. Now I'm in the middle. I was told by the people on top that if I sent this photograph out that I could move up to the top. The people on the top would start acknowledging me and talking to me. It was fascinating the first time I was faced with this to have that conversation. So they're forming their own social groups and social levels. (Massachusetts, J1, Other Adult Focus Group)

Other adults spoke strongly about the ways teens actively engaged in working out social status within and across peer groups, and they used the social and communicative tools available to them to meet these ends. The teen years, it appears, are a critical time to develop knowledge of power and control in one-to-one and group relationships. This work is in preparation for living as an adult in communities and work environments where one must exercise these skills.

Sex, and Not Sex, as Motivations for Sexting

Sexual motivations for sexting ranged from the desire for sex to the desire to avoid real sex. Adults were aware that both play a role in adolescents' thinking.

Flirtation is the 'getting the feet wet stage' of a sexual encounter, and adults believed sexting plays many roles in the process of flirtation. In a focus group in Massachusetts, Ms. Norman said, "I think it's a form of the way they flirt back and forth with each other," a statement enlarged upon by Mr. O'Donnell.

> Mr. O'Donnell: And unfortunately, they've upped it about ten notches with the content of it. I don't think kids today know how to communicate their feelings. And you know, 'Well, I like that person, so I'll send them a picture of me, or I'll say something dirty, and they'll think it's funny, and they'll think I'm funny, and that's how I'll get them.' I don't think, they don't process the whole. (Massachusetts, S1, Other Adult Focus Group)

Mr. O'Donnell demonstrated the many perspectives an adult brings to the consideration of teen motivations, from attention-getting and communication to the impact of the broadcast technology.

For teens, geography, access to transportation, and age may make face-to-face sexual encounters difficult, but sexting can bridge those distances.

> Ms. Polk: I think it's very common. And I feel that way because, the teens they're involved in relationships, and as an adult, you can just go, and you're more flexible about seeing the person, if you're in a relationship with a person. But as a teen, the sexting part, 'I can't get to you, but this is a way that we can stay in touch, and communicate, and be in this relationship.' (South Carolina, Norton, Educator Group)

In such instances, sexting is a means of sexual expression and connection that can be conducted from different locations.

Shifting from views on what kind of sex is sexting, there were also views on what kind of sex it is not. Ms. Martinez provided a provocative perspective on the not-sex notion of sexting.

> Ms. Martinez: Every comment that I've been hearing just makes absolute sense to me. And the one thing that keeps coming into my mind every time I hear you guys speak is to me, it's almost like these teens might be using this as a way of I'm not having sex with them. I'm just sending them a picture. You know, if cybersex is OK, why isn't sexting OK? You know, you've heard and seen of all this cybersex that goes on. I'm not really having sex with someone, I'm not a slut. You know, because I'm not having sex with all these guys. I'm just sending them a picture. So what's a picture? So I feel like it's in their mind … it's like well, I'm not going that extra step and actually sleeping with

them. It's just a picture until it leaks. (Massachusetts, A1, Other Adult Focus Group)

While others have interpreted the use of sexting as an alternative to intercourse and the issues of pregnancy and sexually transmitted diseases, Ms. Martinez suggested that sexting, when it is construed as not real sex, allows a girl to explore sexuality with a wide range of men but will prevent her from actually being a slut, the term that applied to girls having sex with a number of individuals. Unfortunately, the term slut, as was uncovered in this study, was easily applied to girls who are publicly exposed to be sexting.

Sexting as Accidental or Happenstance

> Mr. Quirk: It's easy, it's attention getting, they're bored, it's a way to bully, and I think some do it because they have low self-esteem and they don't know any other way to communicate. (South Carolina, Admin Focus Group, Brad)

Mr. Quirk expressed a commonly held view of those in the Other Adult category and that is that boredom, wed with opportunity and need, can lead to sexting. This viewpoint was enlarged upon by Ms. Ransom, who took the notion a step further as she worried about sexting as an act without connection to a meaningful romantic attachment.

> Ms. Ransom: Again, the kids and the adults, they use that, there are no social skills behind it. So if there are no social skills they don't know anything about romance because you have to be able to be social to romance someone. So they don't know anything about either one so when they do it a lot of times it's something to do. I send you a picture with your telephone because now smart phones, you can attach the picture to the telephone number. So I text you, my picture shows up regardless of what kind of picture I send and a lot of times they can be misconstrued. A person does not know in what context you used a sentence or how you say it. They just see the word. And it's very scary to me. (Ohio, Other Adult Focus Group 1)

Ms. Ransom's comments raised an issue that many adults were concerned about, and that is social or communication skills. For many adults, discussions about social practices and communication were often conflated with worries about technology (the Internet, cell phones, texting, and email communication), developing into a chicken or egg dilemma: Which came first? Deteriorating social skills or the rise of the cell phone and Internet? What is having an effect on what? As was demonstrated here, the question of what kind of sex is sexting quickly drew participants into consideration of a range of social discourses they saw as related and interacting one upon the other.

Blame the Technology

Adults strongly believed that cell phones with storage and broadcast capacity, to name just a few of the affordances of these tools, have completely changed aspects of teen relationships and interactions. Today's teens routinely use or scan the cell phone contents of others, as these two illustrations from Ms. O'Neil in a South Carolina focus group demonstrated.

> Ms. O'Neil: I think too that it could even be that let's say you're in a relationship with someone. Well, that person could have friends who get your phone. And the person who you sent the picture to may not send it to anyone else. But if you know, he or she's at a friend house, and the other person gets inside it. You know, once it's there, it's there. And it can make it out there in a matter of seconds.
> Ms. O'Neil: Yeah, or you know, just a guy gets another guy's phone, and it'd be funny to send this all to so and so. And you know, I guess it's that easy. (South Carolina, Wes, Other Adult Focus Group)

Cell phones are ubiquitous in our culture, and they are loaded with many kinds of personal information. These qualities of cell phones are now commonplace understandings within all ranks of society, including youth.

GENDER AND THE CHARACTERISTICS OF YOUTH WHO WOULD OR WOULD NOT SEXT

In the Other Adult focus groups, participants were asked: What are the characteristics of youth who would or would not engage in sexting? Subsequently we probed them about the ways gender and age might play a factor in sexting.

Boys Who Would Sext

Adults described boys as being clueless in many of the relationship areas and, in truth, more interested in their own body image. Boys were seen to be active in asking, soliciting, initiating, and pressuring girls for pictures. They enjoy collecting photos, and will forward and share with others to demonstrate what they have in their collection. Terms like bragging, conquering, and hormones were used in relationship to boys' sexting behavior. Boys anticipate, rightly or wrongly, that receiving a photo from a girl may be the gateway to more sexual favors. What was particularly interesting was that when adults made the connection of sexting to pornography, they associated it much more with boys than with girls.

> Ms. Lawrence: I don't know that I can answer that because like this gentleman was talking about, with the statistics varying, I don't have any sense of how often girls are doing it, versus how [often boys] are doing it. If I had some sense, I could probably answer that. I'm sitting here thinking though, like about adult pornography, it's always been very male-oriented, you've got your Playboys, your Penthouse, blah, blah. I can't think of one that's made for women. I guess there's a Playboy, I don't know. Playgirl, I guess there is, but sort of historically it's always been kind of like guys were into that thing, and women were not, who they were targeting with these magazines. I have a feeling, if you were to look at real numbers, it's probably girls doing it more. Boys are receiving it, but I bet the girls are taking the clothes off, and taking pictures of them naked. So that would be my guess. (Massachusetts, J2, Other Adult Focus Group)

Ms. O'Connor distinguished gendered sexting behavior in this way:

> Ms. O'Connor: For females, it's much more targeted, much more an issue of power that they have, as opposed to boys, it might just be a macho thing. For girls, it's much more calculated. (Massachusetts, SE2, Other Adult Focus Group)

This illustration pits girls (the calculating ones) against boys (just a macho thing), implying that macho lacks calculation, thus, placing it in the clueless or benign category.

Girls Who Would Sext

Adults in these groups saw girls' engagement in sexting as related to a drive for love, attention, and that one special person. They often look at sexting as a sign of intimacy, and they are hopeful their trust will be reciprocated.

> Ms. Lappen: Every year I tell the story about Oprah. There's two, 14-year-olds holding hands, and they're all in love. And they pulled out from the guy how long they think that they would be together. He said a long time. And then Oprah pushed him, how long is a long time? And they're holding hands and looking at each other lovingly, and then the guy says I don't know, six months to a year? So the girl drops his hand. And so my entire class, always I do it every year when I'm teaching Romeo and Juliet. We talk about this. And every year all the girls are you know, wide-eyed and the guys are looking at me like I just killed all their game. (laughter) And I think that has to do with you know, girls especially think that they can trust this person because they're in love with them, and they love them back. And that this will never get anywhere, but they don't have the foresight just like we were talking about yesterday, or the vision to know that the future will hold a completely different thing. And they won't be able to trust that person … with their information. (South Carolina, Wes, Other Adult Focus Group)

Ms. Lappen, like many adults, was aware that male and female perspectives can differ widely in regard to romantic relationships.

Based on the coding of data in the Other Adult category, girls who would sext were also described as aggressive, boy crazy, sexual beings, and confident. They could also be viewed as acting out of motivations of insecurity, low self-esteem, and being emotionally needy.

> Mr. Montgomery: I will put it this way, girls are boy crazy, so they'll do anything to impress a guy. And guys want to be players. So if they have 30 pictures on there from 30 different girls and they show their buddies, like hey man, look at all these pictures I got. And the girls are you know, group huddle. I want to get this boy, I like this boy, I want him to like me. Then five other girls are thinking the same thing, they'll do whatever it takes. (South Carolina, Wes, Other Adult Focus Group)

Sexting, as described by Mr. Montgomery, is almost a team sport, in which males and females in different peer groups are engaged in active competition.

Who Are the Youth Who Do Not Sext?

At the same time adults believed sexting is very common, collectively they appeared to have a clear, sharp picture of the young person who is not engaged in sexting. Young people who will be going to college for specific careers and are seen as highly motivated and self-confident, regardless of gender, were believed to have the wherewithal to withstand peer pressure and requests for photos or inappropriate sexual involvement. These young people were seen as having the defense mechanisms in place that would guard them from this sort of sexual activity.

> Ms. Lewis: You see it through all perspectives. In the high school, you see the smart kids who are really, really smart, and you see the kids that, you know, everybody is everybody. And you see them all doing it in some form or another. And I do think there's a focus on some where you see some with the low self-esteem, they'll get someone that says oh, you know, this is what I want to do, and if you do this, I'll date you something like that. I think they're more susceptible to it than some of the others. Some of the others have … defense mechanisms. But when you have low self-esteem, they think that's something that's going to make them more popular, and that's really key I think in high school is they want to be popular, so they do whatever is necessary. (Ohio: Educator Group 3)

From this perspective, gender was not as important a predictor of sexting engagement as was a positive sense of the present and future.

WHO WILL GUIDE YOUNG PEOPLE IN THEIR NEED FOR INFORMATION ABOUT SEXUALITY, INTIMACY, AND GENDER?

In the Other Adult category, the participants' roles were a critical marker in distinguishing the views one possessed in relationship to this question. The roles of focus group members differed by institution (school, legal system, or community organization) and by position within that institution (administrator or assistant, educator or enforcer). Moreover, institutions were not homogeneous across regional areas; that is, Ohio differed from

South Carolina and from Massachusetts, and there were also significant differences within as well as across regional areas in the individual cultures of communities and institutions. There were also differences in the beliefs of particular professional areas—educators are inculcated with different perspectives than attorneys, and guidance counselors may have different training from police officers or community youth workers. As described above, age (a foot in both camps—before and after the birth of the Internet) may play a significant role in how an individual approaches this question, as may gender.

That being said, there are some larger generalizations that can be made about the views of those in the Other Adult category. A striking commonality was the way educators felt pressured to meet what they saw as the legitimate goals or objectives of formal education—to instruct youth in specific content areas and to demonstrate achievement or competence of knowledge in these areas—while at the same time they are asked to address character issues and emerging issues like sexting.

> Ms. Lifton: As someone who works with the curriculum and I have to follow the fidelity of my curriculum, there's really not a lot of wiggle room for me to include this topic, which is really unfortunate because since I teach sexual health and teen pregnancy prevention and STD [Sexually Transmitted Diseases] prevention and it's a huge component that should really be addressed alongside of that. But unless a student asks me to address something or discloses something I can't address it because of the nature of the type of curriculum I work with. So I think moving forward as a health educator when we're looking to implement programs we should really be looking to implement a variety of [topics] we include—teen dating violence I think that should be included certainly with that. (Ohio, Educator, Focus Group 2)

Ms. Lifton described the struggle she has to include a new topic, sexting, into the health curriculum where she feels it legitimately belongs. In many schools, there is not a specific place for topics like sexting. Ms. Lappen described a sexting education session that happened as a kind of accident.

> Ms. Lappen: I went to an extremely informative session with our SRO [School Resource Officer] officer beginning of the year where they split up the classes. And it was just with seniors though, I believe. I'm not sure if our entire school went, but … the kids have never paid closer attention to anything, [not] that I've ever

seen. And they were extremely into it, and I think this message should be delivered frequently, if not once a semester to our entire student body. And the only reason we did that is because it was a random day we needed to fill with activities. And so we brought somebody in. It wasn't during testing. You know, it's not a common thing. But they were asking questions, then you could see light bulbs going off, and they were thinking. (South Carolina, Wes, Educator Group)

Even though most in the Other Adult category were also parents themselves, in their roles within an institution many also blamed parents as the culprits who were unable or unwilling to successfully discipline youth sexual (and gendered) behavior. While those in the Other Adult category acknowledged the good and responsible parents, they complained that many parents just don't get it, do not monitor their children carefully enough, don't respond appropriately to complaints from school, and are not providing good role models. They were concerned that many parents feel matters are out of control and are overwhelmed by the changes wrought by the Internet and changing social practices. As Mr. Stanton, a School Resource Officer (SRO) made clear, parents and school educators may both be struggling with these issues.

Mr. Stanton: I work in law enforcement and I have seen the shock factor first hand, and it is incredible. Some of them even go back in their seats. But I think two people were saying earlier I think that you've had parents that in many ways are wonderful parents, and are very good people, but they don't get it. And you have educators too that are excellent educators, but they don't get it. By the time stuff gets to law enforcement, it's ballooned so out of control ... and I see this a lot. In particular with educators when you have parents hammering them, saying what's gonna be done, what are you doing about this. Let me refer to the SRO. Let me give you his information. I think that it's really a combination of the kids, but also the good parents that just don't get it and the excellent educators that just don't get it. (Massachusetts, J1 Other Adult Focus Group)

CONCLUSIONS

The tri-focal lens used by adults in the Other Adult category to view youth and their sexting activities is at once fracturing and synthesizing. It is fracturing in that they see youth and their issues from multiple perspectives—the many roles and institutions they occupy—and from different temporal standpoints: who they have been, who they are, and where they imagine the future is heading. The tri-focal lens is synthesizing in that adults in this category are examining the same objects with many of the same attitudes. As such, they share a common nostalgia about time—past, present, and future—that is inextricably linked to the ways they perceive youth actions in regard to relationships, sexuality, and gendered concerns. Ms. Urbine's reflection on youth, sexuality, and education seems particularly fitting as the final word on this topic, as it is highly representative of the ways adults drew together multiple discourses as they sought to make sense of these topics.

> Ms. Urbine: I find it interesting how we, as a culture, have allowed sexuality to become such a part of our every day, and then we're surprised that our children are using this in our technology. So, I mean, you know, anybody that watches the Super Bowl, or any kind of, you know—there's—I don't even know what the name of it is, there's some website, and the ladies are like, almost—GoDaddy, there it is. I mean, so you look at things like that, and then we're surprised that our children are using the technology. They are so much more sexualized than we, the generation before them, and the generation before them, and I think we're pretty represented in this room right here, that we find it offensive, and we find it to be, you know, wrong, when in fact, we encourage it by allowing our children to exist in this culture. I mean, unless you're going to put them in a cave. So, my perspective is, is teaching to it. Teaching respect, and understanding of what they're experiencing, social mistakes. You know, when we made social mistakes as teenagers, and I'll just use me for example, five people might have known that. Today, 500 people know. We're making the same mistakes, it's just that because of our technology, because it's so much more broad, more people know about our mistakes. (Ohio, Other Adult Focus Group)

Ms. Urbine was sympathetic to young people and eager to support them to follow safer paths, but at the same time she felt technology and our sexualized society are much to blame for the presence of sexting. And, as has been noted before, her example of sexual inappropriateness focused on the female gender.

SECTION II: CONCLUSION

COMPARING THE VIEWS OF ADULTS

In closing this section on the adult data, I will compare the views of caregivers or parents on the one hand with those in the Other Adult category on the other hand, providing a context from which to consider adult views in relationship to youth views. There is much similarity in perspective among all adults, and yet there are also significant contrasts or differences related to role and its opportunities or constraints.

- All adults had difficulty defining sexting, raising many examples of situations they couldn't quite label.
- Overall, adults held a negative perspective on sexting, placing what is problematic about it in the foreground.
- Adults of all stripes shared a fair amount of concern about our changing digital society. They compared the impact of the 1960s and similar social movements with the impact of the Internet, and they were not sure which has been more challenging. Adults discussed the changes in technology in the same breath with raising issues about the increasingly sexualized nature of society.
- In talking about their concerns with the increasingly sexualized nature of society, adults pointed primarily to changes in girls' rather than boys' behavior. Much of their examples related to changes in communication practices (who calls whom; what kind of language one uses) and dress (today's girls were seen to be dressing in much more provocative ways than in the past).
- In considering girls' motivations for sexting, adults believed that sexting is often connected, in girls' minds, to their desire for romance and intimacy, and believed youth and inexperience can lead them astray in this realm. Adults also understood that girls make use of sexting as a tool for reaching social goals, that is, to exercise power and control. Finally, they knew that sexting arises out of the desire for sexual engagement and expression among teens, which they may label as 'hormones,' a kind of shorthand for teen sexuality.
- In regard to boys' motivations for sexting, adults seemed to think boys, more than girls, have a short attention span for the romance motivation. Boys, they believed, were probably more likely to be looking for sexual

experience. Boys were also eager to compare body images and compete for the most masculine and desirable body or the most photos of girls or other sexual accomplishments.

- Adults worried about the hurt that could arise from sexting gone awry, whether from photos, texts, audio, or video. Given the broadcast capacity of Internet and cell phone, they knew this is always a potential hazard. They knew that the hurt would not only occur between a couple, but with the mob mentality all humans possess, that it could easily spread across a peer group and beyond.

- Young people who would sext, regardless of gender, were seen as needier or less self-confident. Young people who would not sext were seen as more confident, probably stronger academically, and less needy.

- Adults appeared to be in agreement with young people that there are gendered differences related to the effects of sexting. In other words, there is a double standard, where girls are considered to be the voting party (girls decide yes or no), while boys are the beseeching party (boys plead and cajole). Also, girls will be more likely to face shame, whereas boys are seen as guilty but less culpable. Girls will be misled by their desire for romance, and boys will be misled by their desire to shine among other boys.

- Adults were surprisingly unaware of the amount of negativity they expressed in regard to youth and youth sexuality, and the nature of that negativity. Safety, control, and compliance with various institutional rules or goals loomed large in their minds. Certainly, they feared for the future and what could happen to youth who were found to be sexting. They spoke with humor, maybe ridicule, about youth aspirations and their romantic engagements. Their conversation about youth (perhaps because it was initiated by discussion of sexting, which is deemed a negative topic), did not depict youth in strong, positive terms, nor did it refer much to youth desire for values, knowledge, or participation in meaningful activity.

- Caretakers or parents were considered by both parent and Other Adult groups to be the single most important variable in teaching positive values and monitoring young people's behavior and digital engagement in order to prevent sexting problems. Ironically, caretakers were also the group with the least access to well-vetted information on teen sexuality and sexting. Their sources were often the media, followed by their children. Those in the Other Adult category had the most opportunity for vetted information on sexuality and sexting through professional development supplied by their organization or profession, but they often struggled with institutional issues related to providing this information to young people.

- Within families, both mothers and fathers were concerned and active in promoting good values and trying to prevent danger from digital avenues; however, the gendered role of parents in this work could be quite different. Males often spoke directly to children around an incident. If the male was more technically astute, he may be assigned a technical monitoring role (although, technically astute females can also take this role). Females were more likely to deal with day-to-day monitoring of technology use and relationship interactions, such as the example where mothers networked together behind the backs of young people to keep on top of problematic behaviors such as sexting.

In the next chapter, I will consider the broader perspective that comes from looking across the four groups—girls, boys, caretakers/parents, and Other Adults—in relationship to each other, as well as the two groups—youth to adults. I will also add the views of others outside the world reflected in the data, to create another contrapuntal theme that will weave through the reflections.

Taken independently, the various points above may not all appear to be speaking directly to the issues of gender and youth sexuality, but as the conversation proceeds it will become evident how beliefs about gendered differences, if present in one argument, will invariably be buried in other discussions about youth and sexuality.

CHAPTER 7

CONCLUSIONS

In regard to gender, teens, and sexuality, five critical findings rose to the fore in the course of this study, which I will discuss in detail in this section. Although I promised this is not a how-to, fix-it book, the discussion of the data and the findings raise important implications about the best ways to support young people to be safe, grow, and prosper as normal, developing sexual beings in a digital world, and I share these recommendations at the end of the chapter

FINDINGS

1. The human curriculum of sexuality is both conserving and adapting. There are components that are hard-wired and others that are soft-wired, and the interaction of the two emerges in context: that is, the variety of physical or natural, social, cultural, and technological circumstances in which humans find themselves.

What is sexting? What is an appropriate expression of one's sexuality? How does gender figure in the sending, receiving, and allocation of consequences? The participants in our study, young and old, debated these questions back and forth. In the case of both youth and adults, technology was ever-present in regard to sexual issues and their communication. Adults spoke with humor of the technologies of the past and the ways these tools were converted to address the sexual needs of their own youth (for instance, the instamatic camera and the Xerox machine). Youth insisted adults had done the same things as they were doing, but claimed adults had forgotten or were embarrassed to say. Both adults and youth spoke of hormones as natural forces no one could deny.

In this study, sexting and sexuality served as the lens for discussions about the processes of conservation and adaption within human society. Although not about sexuality *per se*, the tension humans experience over conserving and adapting is brought to life in a visually stunning mode in the documentary *Home* by Yann Arthus-Bertrand (2009). Modern cities of glass and steel are juxtaposed next to the tents of the surviving nomads on our planet; suburban sprawl contrasts with vast forests and grass lands.

Like those fellow humans portrayed in the film, we too must assemble the human curriculum of sexuality from nature and culture. In the case of sexuality, the curriculum is marked with the restrictions of DNA (nature) and shaped by the considerations of nurture (culture).

The human curriculum of sexuality, made unique by context and technology, continues to unfold for each individual as they move through adolescence. It continues with or without the Internet, cell phones, chat rooms, or video cameras. The human imperative to seek deep intimate contact and to express one's self sexually is still present, whether in the first century or the 21st century (Erickson, 1953/1963).

Along with this imperative comes the approach of full adult responsibilities, including mature sexuality and abiding life relationships with families of various forms. Group connections take many forms in human life, but without doubt, maturity, for many, comes with the establishment of family and the interconnections created between families and larger social groupings (Crockett & Beal, 2012). The curriculum of human sexuality must thus allow for the integration of deep personal, intimate, and sexual relationships with the broader relationships of family and community. Young people must come to understand the subtle nuances of sexuality as it anchors connection. In doing so, they are necessarily engaged in the development of gendered understandings of various kinds (Perry & Pauletti, 2011).

Sexting is just one of the many adaptions sexual expression has made to new technology (Baym, 2010). Through war or peace, tribal or industrial society, sexual expression has been with us, adapting to new times and new technologies. Art historian Esther Pasztory offers a long view of technologies in her thought-provoking book *Thinking with Things: Toward a New Vision of Art* (2005), in which she states,

> Arnold Rubin considered tribal and archaic art to be a form of technology. Masks and figures that are believed to have spirit power are interpreted as agents as active in their societies as microwaves or Walkmans are in ours ... [A]esthetics are the means of technology in archaic type societies ... the first technology of communication and control of humanity. (p.11)

Like all sexual expression, sexting is embedded in unfolding stories, within narratives of romance or despair, hilarity or sadness (Farman, 2014). Shakespeare captured the essential emotions, even if the technologies were different. In today's world, Romeo and Juliet are the young couple desiring each other, but separated by distance and the inability to drive, each sitting in their own bedroom, texting their desire back and forth. In today's world, the confused lovers of *A Midsummer Night's Dream* may be teens wandering the mall on a Friday evening, sending Instagrams from the food court to a clothing store, as young people grab phones out of each other's hands and stare at the contents. In today's world, poor Ophelia might be creating a videoblog as she prepares for the end of life.

2. We are in the midst of a social/technological change that has vast implications for the fundamentals of our cultural notions—temporal, spatial, embodied, and sexual. We are struggling to understand what this will mean for the curriculum of human sexuality and, by extension, our notions of relationship, family, education, and life path.

I was a teen before the Internet and sexting. As the oldest of six, I had to wait for my turn at the single phone sitting in the most public place in my home. Receiving a call from a boy would bring looks and comments from my many siblings, but even more embarrassing was trying to hold a semi-private conversation with said boy in the middle of a large, curious family.

Times have changed and so has the telephone, along with many other technologies. In my college class (Planning, Technology, and School Improvement), for some years I have used a set of TED Talks by Wired Magazine guru Kevin Kelly to introduce students to an historical notion of technology and an understanding of the phenomenal growth of the Internet (Kelly, 2005, 2007, 2009). The TED Talks I have used are now also aging, but they continue to surprise and challenge students' notions of the time and place in which we live and the ways technology is shaping our lives. In 2007, for instance, the Internet was only 5,000 days old and yet it was growing at an exponential rate, connecting all parts of the globe (Kelly, 2007). This kind of rapid change is dizzying when compared to the development and dissemination of, say, the printing press or the wheel!

In my class discussions, similar to what was learned in the sexting study, adults who did not grow up in the digital era, or who came to age at its beginning, struggle with the notions of time and space that are commonplace for younger individuals: being always on, available, and connected to their hive (Hall & Baym, 2011; Baym, 2010). They express surprise as they consider the physical longing many young people feel for their digital gadgets (and the connections these gadgets represent). They are not surprised to hear that there is a phenomenon now dubbed "phantom vibration syndrome" used in discussing the situation of being without your cell phone or imagining it is ringing (Hu, 2013).

Sexting is something digital natives (today's teens) appear to accept whether or not they do it themselves, and this acceptance is true for males and females. Although digital immigrants (many of today's adults) have come to use new digital tools and accept the changed circumstances of our digital times, many express reservations about the impact of these tools, clinging to memories of the ways they think things were before the Internet. They believe sexting is common among adolescents of both genders, but fear the negative results. On the other hand, they know that adults as well as adolescents are sexting. Personally, I am surprised at the number of times I explained to an older adult (someone born before 1970) that I am studying teens and sexting, and their response is, "Well, adults do it too, you know," a response that is often accompanied by a knowing glance, suggesting they know or have heard about people who do. In an example from the larger world, family therapists are now considering the possibilities of sexting for couple's therapy (Parker, Blackburn, Perry & Hawks, 2013).

In looking at adult reservations about then (better times) and now (challenging times), there are several gendered concerns relevant to the focus of this text. In particular, there is the notion expressed by adult participants in our focus groups that the social upheavals of the 1960s, meaning especially the women's movement, are to blame for much of the discomfort adults feel about many issues related to sexuality in our society. What often comes to the fore is their worry that our society is much more sexualized than before the women's movement appeared on the scene.

The evidence they cite for these changes relates to concerns about changes in teen behavior, and invariably it seems, their voices are raised about changes they note in girls' behavior. They find fault with girls for the way they talk, dress, and engage in flirtations and other sexual activities. Overall, girls are thought to be far more aggressive than they were before (meaning before the speaker's own adolescence). Girls' aggressiveness is seen to be highly sexual in nature. Again, I am surprised at the number of times older adults say, "Aren't the girls just too much today!" or "The girls have gotten so much more aggressive," when I reveal that I am studying teens and sexting. Nothing is said about changed sexual behavior of boys. Does that mean there has not been a change in their behavior? Or does it mean that the change in girls' behavior is most worthy of note?

This perspective on boys' issues is well represented by Dennis Rainey, founder and writer for *FamilyLife*, a Christian help website, in an article titled "Protecting Your Son from Aggressive Girls" (2008). The subtitle or introductory sentence from this article is: "We're seeing a surge in girls taking the initiative with guys at younger and younger ages, and aggressively attempting to lure them into sexual activity." Rainey, a man who had previously written a book on interviewing daughters' dates, wrote this subsequent article when he became aware that sexually aggressive girls were putting boys at peril. I mention this piece not to promote or criticize Rainey or the Christian viewpoint, nor to argue with the notion that girls are more or less sexually aggressive today. Rather, this is a piece that rings very true to the comments I have received on this topic.

Regardless of whether this hypothesis is true or not, what are the effects of this particular critique of adolescent girls, I wonder? How will it shape teen girls' futures? How is it simultaneously shaping different futures for boys? How does it shape justice and decision-making about young people? Emerging research on adolescent narrative development points to the extremely important role adults play in shaping youth identity and future perspectives through narrative scaffolding, reason enough to be concerned about the unexamined nature of the narratives regarding gender and sexuality to which we are exposing youth (McLean & Mansfield, 2012).

Consideration of the gendered critique of adolescents voiced in the pages of this text has brought me to the understanding that the women's movement (and by extension the men's movement) has only begun to unfold within our society. Women's suffrage, legislation for equal pay opportunities, etc., all of these are significant steps for women, but they signify the infancy of gender reorganization and renewal in a global digital age, and we have so much further to go. The current anxieties about gender are an expression of the first waves of change, but as discussed in the next section, there are still deeply significant changes to be made.

I was greatly surprised to learn from this study how complicit adult women are in this criticism of girls. I don't know why this surprised me, but it did. I wanted them to stick up for girls, but that wasn't happening. It was as if they felt betrayed by young women who were not following the rules they had been made to follow in their youth, however painful it may have been to them. This suggests to me that next steps in the movement for gender equality will have to look not just outward to legislation and judicial change, but also inward to examine the hopes, fears, jealousies, and assumptions that hamper progress.

3. Despite the overt changes in gendered expectations in many realms of our society, many older patterns persist covertly. In particular, we continue the pattern in which boys suffer guilt for sexual missteps, but girls suffer shame. This difference has significant implications for the possibilities of youth and their future lives.

Girls and boys differentiate themselves in terms of motivations for sexting. Girls prioritize romance, followed by emphasis on peer social control, and lastly sex. Boys prioritize competition (peer social control), then sex, and romance comes in third. These gendered priorities mix and match within individuals and various social groups. Despite these individual and group differences, however, the larger gendered pattern is discernable: girls emphasize romance like a parasol of respectability, and boys emphasize bragging rights similar to the fully spread peacock's tail.

Adults' beliefs about teen motivations for sexting appear to fall along similar lines. However, adults appear to discount youth capacity for romantic or deep/personal relationships. They appear to believe the problematic issues of sexual encounter are the ones that deserve their attention. They pay surprisingly little attention to the positive role they as adults might play supporting youth to develop deep, meaningful relationships with potential partners. In truth, researchers believe we know relatively little about adolescents' romantic relationships (Cook, Buehler, & Blair, 2013).

A highly significant issue that was identified in this research is the ways girls and boys are also differentiated in regard to consequences: boys suffer guilt for sexual missteps, but girls suffer shame (Brown, 2010). This is not to say that boys cannot be shamed. For instance in this study, boys describe being shamed for being physically inadequate (having a small penis) or failing to attract cute women. However, the deck is stacked against girls who make a sexual misstep, and shame is the primary tool with which they are brought to heel.

Shame is leveraged against girls on multiple levels. Once initiated, it can come from peers, parents, teachers, administrators, and other community members. Its effects are deep and penetrating. Researchers of shame have found it to be strongly connected to issues of addiction and suicide (Brown, 2010, 2012). As a boy in this study said, "A girl can suicide."

Our findings in this area align closely with the phenomenon described as slut-shaming, an established term in the area of human sexuality. Wikipedia describes it as, "… a neologism used to describe the act of making a person, especially a woman, feel guilty or inferior for sexual behaviors or desires that deviate from traditional or orthodox gender expectations …" ("Slut-shaming," n.d.). In a British study of teens and sexting, Ringrose and her colleagues uncovered results very similar to ours, in which the male competition for images creates "… a hierarchical economy of value around looking and desiring in the school culture" (Ringrose et al., 2013, p. 315). Tanenbaum, in a much earlier work (1999), identified similar gendered issues.

Another concern this study brings forward is that adults, in focusing on sexting and sex, may be overlooking serious issues of class and power.

Both boys and girls referred to the ways sex and relationship behaviors (including sexting) are often aimed at gaining improved social standing, peer control or disciplining. Sex and power are demonstrated to have close linkages, and sexting, too, can serve these ends. Young people debate: if I send this photo will I gain access to this popular person and improve my status? If I send this photo will my enemy be vanquished? They grab each other's phones and comb over the photos that are stored there; who has more? Who has photos of whom? How sexual are the photos?

A recent study led by Elizabeth Armstrong of the University of Michigan provides strong evidence that class critique, more than sexual critique, is at the heart of slut-shaming activities, at least among college age women. Affluent women label women whom they identify as trashy (of lower class) as sluts, while less affluent women label those they deem to be social climbers as sluts (Bahadur, 6/2/14).

The incident of the flip described in the chapter on boys' perspectives raises serious questions about the ways class and gender are worked to the advantage of some and the great disadvantage of others. In the situation of the flip, boys and girls describe how a girl becomes a member of a kind of untouchable class—vulnerable women on the edge of the sex trades. I would argue that the flip represents the seasoning sequence of sexual trafficking, in which recruits are culled out from the general group based upon an evaluation of their neediness. These recruits are then systematically seduced and integrated into a new, marginalized position within society. I see a strong connecting thread between the labels that are blithely applied among adolescents and others (slut, whore, easy) as a means of shaming girls to bring about compliance and the category of women who are designated flip or prostitute (Davidson, 2014).

The gendered consequences of sexual missteps are deeply ingrained in our society. Shame, not guilt, leads to a specific kind of gendered exploitation and marginalization within society. The maintenance of a permanent class of women who are marked for sexual exploitation has deep, historical roots. Susan Griffin writes of the role of courtesans in Greek society and later European society. In France, for instance, most women entered this work as a grisette (a term originally meaning milliner), one who combined prostitution with other forms of work. Grisettes were at the bottom of the prostitutional pyramid. Above them came the lorette, who were fully supported by prostitutional activities, and finally the tiny few who were recognized as courtesans and lavishly supported by one, and often many patrons. Under this scheme, the flip most resembles the grisette, a woman who is stepping into the first rung of this marginalized positioning for women (Griffin, 2001, 2011).

Whether in the past or today, the key conditions that lead to entry on this path are an overwhelming need of some sort in a woman's life that requires resources she cannot obtain by other means—whether these be economic, physical or emotional (US Department of State, 2008). This is the opening for exploitation or the notion of the fall from good society, a theme that has been the focus of many pieces from English literature. In this vein, I am always reminded of Jane Austen's *Pride and Prejudice* and the pre-occupations of the 19th century characters with finding safe partners in the midst of many dangerous (sexual) choices. In this tale, women who make sexual missteps are lost to society; witness the fate of Lydia, who goes off with the wicked military officer Wickham. In doing so, the sexual misconduct of one sister affects the entire family, threatening to derail the futures of the good (sexually controlled) sisters, and only heroic action from Mr. Darcy finally saves the family from total shame (Davidson, Thompson & Harris, 2014).

It bears repeating that although the example of the flip is drawn from the African-American community in South Carolina, it should not be assumed that such issues are solely confined to the African-American community or to the South. As the various historical examples demonstrate, the creation and maintenance of a separate class of women who can be used for sexual purposes is known to many, many communities. Unquestionably, it is disturbing is to find evidence of such things occurring in American high schools in the 21st century.

The findings about the conserving features of gender revealed by this study are also troubling to me in uniquely personal ways. Writing about them brings me back to my adolescence and memories of shame. As a white child in an inter-racial household, my stepfather a black jazz musician, I experienced my own version of the story of the flip. In the late 1960s and early 1970s, these racial facts were circumstances ripe for identifying me as a girl who could be sexually exploited. I didn't have to do anything, I was classified despite myself. When I write about the flip, I feel the shame I was exposed to decades ago, and I know it to be true: the gendered system is still working as it was laid out to work.

4. Adults are pointing the fingers of blame in many directions from the various silos in which they locate themselves: home, school, or community. Their abdication of responsibility for the curriculum of human sexuality leaves adolescents without access to important information and relationships through which to build their lives into the future.

Youth have reservations about adult ability or desire to address youth needs and concerns regarding sexuality and technology. Their reservations are part youthful impertinence, part reference to the gap between digital native and immigrant, and part truth—the sad truth that we are failing youth in their need for information and guidance about sexuality, intimacy, and the importance of relationship.

The adults we spoke to were youth advocates and certainly did not want youth to be hurt or damaged, but adult parties feel constraints based on the roles and positions they occupy. Parents feel overwhelmed by the responsibility of overseeing the development of teen sexuality with the added technological layer. Adults in schools and other situations beg off with, "It's not my job." Or "They expect us to do everything. There just isn't enough time." Everyone blames parents, even other parents.

It is true that as high stakes testing and the standards movement has swung into high gear, the emphasis in schools has shifted to achievement over relationship, goals in place of values. Some of the results are good; there is pressure to ensure that every student achieves. Technologies, too, have been important in improving schools. Parents and teachers now talk more frequently, text, and share information about homework. But some of the effect is regrettable; youth have lost important access to adult figures during their teen years. The environment of high school is much more pressurized, competitive, and intense.

While this finding is dissatisfying, it was reassuring to hear what youth, in particular, had to say about the way change could be achieved. Debbie provided a good example of some of this feedback:

> Debbie: I think that it would definitely help if other teenagers talked to other teenagers about it, just because I think that they would be able to directly relate more, but I also think just having your parents talk about it, and I also think people should just talk about it more at school, because I think it's just getting swept under the rug and people are just kind of trying to ignore it, and sex ed and everything helps and that's great, but I don't think that's good enough anymore, because technology is advancing so fast, and it's not just having sex and just hooking up with people, there's a technological aspect to it now, and sex ed doesn't cover that, and so I think as technology gets better and changes, everything else has to adapt to that because otherwise it's not going to be good. (Ohio: Norse)

It is also gratifying to recognize that professionals in a number of fields also recognize this dilemma and are organizing to attend carefully to the complex considerations at the confluence of teens, sexuality, gender, and digital media (e.g., Hua, 2012).

5. The media—a nebulous yet powerful force working within our society—does much to inform, discipline, and help us to recast our understanding of gender, youth, and sexuality. Is it friend or foe in the struggle to build healthy, sexual adolescents?

The media is a powerful force across society, from the older fashioned broadcasting mode to the newer forms of social media, interactively global and local (or glocal as it is now described). Teens and adults described many forms of media encounter with sexting—on talk shows, newscasts, in movies, the tweets of celebrities, and newspaper articles. Some of these encounters were formal reporting from so-called authorized sources, but there were many personal forms of reporting, such as the celebrity tweet, followed by retweets and shares that landed in Facebook entries or texts from friends. Information came in the form of non-fiction and fiction (novel, movie, and story themes).

When teens and adults referred to the media coverage of sexting, they also raised issues about the overall notion of sexuality projected in media; in other words, how are boys and girls depicted as developing, sexual beings? As mentioned above, adults find the world to be a more sexualized place and, in particular, they find girls to be far more sexualized than in the past.

Whether or not this is true, this is the impression they have of the media, and impressions are important truths simply by their presence. How might a more thoughtful and caring view of youth, their development, and the human curriculum of sexuality on the part of broadcasters, social casters, and other media outlets, lead to more thoughtful reporting on and portrayal of youth and concerns about youth? Who would take the lead on such a movement?

Teens made strong points about the ways media messages could provide better information about issues relating to sexting.

> Brad: Hey [they] even have commercials for Viagra. OK, you can replace some of those with commercials on sexting. (South Carolina: Wes)

RECOMMENDATIONS FOR PRACTICE

The five findings from the study suggest a suite of specific recommendations that, if put into practice, would do much to improve the lives of youth, families, and those who work with and for youth.

1. Sexuality and gender are key components of healthy adolescent development. They lay the groundwork for future capacity to participate fully as a family member or parent, a friend, good co-worker or community leader. If this is true, then it stands to reason that society needs to pay close attention to the human curriculum of sexuality, particularly as it unfolds during the teen years. This suggests a preventative, rather than a punitive, approach to working with youth.

2. Parents, those who work with youth, and youth themselves, need assistance to develop a perspective on technology that recognizes its role across time in human society, a perspective that will allow us to make proactive, rather than reactive, use of technology in support of healthy youth development and, in particular, the curriculum of human sexuality (Brown, Keller, & Stern, 2009).

3. Negative gender assumptions, prejudices, and restrictions are a matter of concern to all human beings. These issues affect everyone, regardless of their gendered identification. It is critical that we continue to identify gendered issues that negatively impact different groups and demonstrate the willingness to critique and address these concerns on all fronts.

4. All adults must claim responsibility for moving forward a positive agenda to support healthy youth development. Unity across roles, rather than isolation within roles, will provide youth with the best opportunities. From the family to the neighborhood, from the school to the community, are we doing what needs to be done to help youth develop to their full potential as human beings? Do our efforts make sense and have relevance to the needs of youth in a digital society?

5. I do not seek to trample on the Bill of Rights, but media conglomerates of various sorts must bear responsibility for promoting an agenda supportive of healthy adolescent development within their organization and across their various products, as well as supporting work to tailor technological solutions to protecting youth. They wield immense power as informants and opinion makers, and it behooves them to use this power to support teens' healthy development.

CAVEATS AND CONSIDERATIONS

I would like to raise three areas of concern for readers and/or future researchers: 1) sampling beyond the heteronormative, 2) consideration of gender and teens in regard to class and power, and 3) recognition of adult gender impact.

Ours was a self-selected and apparently primarily heteronormative sample. What about gay, lesbian, bisexual, and transgendered youth? There were very few references to them in our focus groups. How are they participating in these technological changes? How do these views of sexuality and the human sexual curriculum pertain to them, their search for sexual identity, and their desire for sexual expression? These are questions that cannot be answered by this study but should be taken up by other researchers.

Secondly, the questions of gender and teens raised here are deeply entangled with issues of class and power, which are doubly entangled with considerations of race, religion, culture, and ethnicity (e.g. Cunningham, Swanson, & Hayes, 2013; Landry, Gonzales, Wood & Vyas, 2013). These issues need to be thoughtfully considered when trying to decipher issues of gender and difference in regard to teens. It was not possible to give these considerations ample time and space in this book, but they are critical concerns with which we must wrestle.

In line with this self-critique, I would also suggest that this text, while carefully distinguishing between male and female youth, does not pay adequate attention to the significance of the effect of adults' gender (and adult assumptions based on their gendered perspectives), and yet this may be a highly important variable (Root & Denham, 2010).

THE LAST WORDS

This text speaks in many tongues: the voices of girls and boys, mothers, and fathers; the words of teachers, social workers, and attorneys. These individuals live in diverse parts of the United States—the Northeast, South, and Midwest. I thank them all for sharing their thoughts about sexting and teens and, by extension, gender, technology, and the challenges of growing up in today's world. Within these words are touches of tenderness, swathes of anxiety, and bursts of laughter.

The human curriculum of sexuality as it is represented in the focus groups is alive and well. Romance is here in abundance, whether it be engagement (flirting, dating, becoming intimate) or its opposite—breaking up (arguing, detaching, or even acting out). Likewise, there is much here in regard to social relationships of all sorts: boys being boys, girls being girls, and the ways boys' and girls' desires weave around each other. Adults of all sorts are seen contemplating and interacting with the lives of youth and trying to explain and shape better outcomes.

Not surprisingly, there is also sadness and fear to be found here, in the form of marginalization, rejection or loss. There is also danger for youth (male or female who can be trapped and lost) and for adults (who might make bad decisions, or fail to protect youth).

As described here, the human curriculum of sexuality unfolds within the context of families, playgrounds, and malls, as well as schools, courts, police, and juvenile justice systems. In all of these places, youth are exploring gender, developing a sense of their gendered selves, and preparing to enter the adult world as adults with gendered identities and understandings. In a digital world, this work makes use of many forms of digital technology, from cell phones and computers to digital photos and text messaging. The digital forms rapidly multiply and change, but they are still held to the standard of human needs for communication, intimacy, and interaction (e.g., Weisskirch & Delevi, 2012).

Youth and adults expressed excitement and doubts about the future of our digital world. Sexting is only one of the many challenges facing teens as they explore the possibilities of intimacy and involvement. It is my hope that by taking the time to explore the knotty complications of digital sexuality, we have also gained insight into gender as it unfolds in teen lives—and by doing so, I hope we have brought some light and possibility to the issues facing the young people of our changing world.

REFERENCES

Ahmed, S. (2006). *Queer phenomenology: Orientations, objects, and others.* Durham, NC: Duke University Press.

Arthus-Bertrand, Y. (Director). (2009). *Home*: Distributed by Twentieth Century Fox Home Entertainment.

Bahadur, N. (2014, June 2). Slut-shaming is more about class than sexual activity, study finds. *Huffington Post.* Retrieved June 30, 2014, from http://www.huffingtonpost.com/2014/06/02/slutshaming-isnt-related-sexual-activity_n_5418711.html

Baym, N. K. (2010). *Personal connections in the digital age.* Cambridge, UK: Polity Press.

Bazelon, E. (2013). *Sticks and stones: Defeating the culture of bullying and rediscovering the power of character and empathy.* New York: Random House.

boyd, d. (2014). *It's complicated: The social lives of networked teens.* New Haven: Yale University Press.

Brown, B. (2010). *The gifts of imperfection: Let go of who you think you're supposed to be and embrace who you are.* Center City, MI: Hazelden. (Audiobook).

Brown, B. (2012). *Men, women, and worthiness: The experience of shame and the power of being enough.* Retrieved from http://www.soundstrue.com/shop/Men,-Women,-and-Worthiness/4120.pd

Brown, J., Keller, S., & Stern, S. (2009). Sex, sexuality, sexting, and sexed: Adolescents and the media. *The Prevention Researcher, 16(4) 12-16.* Retrieved from http://www.tpronline.org/article.cfm/ Sex_Sexuality_Sexting_and_SexEd

Brunker, M. (2009, January 16). 'Sexting' surprise: Teens face child porn charges. Retrieved from http://www. msnbc.msn.com/id/ 28679588/

Butler, J. (2008). *Gender trouble.* NY: Routledge Press.

Cisneros, C., & Davidson, J. (2012). Qualitative computing and qualitative research: Addressing the challenges of technology and globalization. *Forum: Qualitative Social Research (FQS), 13*(2), Art 15. Retrieved from http://www.qualitative-research.net/index.php/fqs/article/view/1853

Connected Learning. (n.d.). Retrieved July 14, 2014, from connectedlearning.tv

Cook, E. C., Buehler, C., & Blair, B. L. (2013). Adolescents' emotional reactivity across relationship contexts. *Developmental Psychology, 49*(2), 341-352. doi: 10.1037/a0028342

Cox Communications, Inc. (2009). *Teen online & wireless safety survey: Cyberbullying, sexting, and parental controls.* Cox Communications in Partnership with the National Center for Missing & Exploited Children (NCMEC).

Crockett, L., & Beal, S. (2012). The life course in the making: Gender and the development of adolescents' expected timing of adult role transitions. *Developmental Psychology, 48*(6), 1727-1738. doi: 10.1037/a0027538

Cunningham, M., Swanson, D. P., & Hayes, D. M. (2013). School- and community-based associations to hypermasculine attitudes in African American adolescent males. *American Journal of Ortho-psychiatry, 83*(2 Pt 3), 244-251. doi: 10.1111/ajop.12029

Davidson, J. (2003). A new role in facilitating school reform: The case of the educational technologist. *Teachers College Record, 105*(5), 729-752.

Davidson, J. (2014a). *Adolescent girls and the orientation of gender: Initiation of a dialogue between Sara Ahmed's* Queer Phenomenology *and teen girls' musings on the topic of sexting.* Paper presented at the UML Gender Studies Conference, February 2014, University of Massachusetts-Lowell, MA.

Davidson, J. (2014b). Bruce's magnificent quartet: Inquiry, community, technology, and literacy—Implications for renewing qualitative research in the 21st century. *E-learning and Digital Media, 11(5).*

Davidson, J. (2014c). *The flip: A narrative of gendered violence in a study of adolescence and sexting.* Paper presented at the 2014 International Conference on Narrative, March 27-30, 2014, Massachusetts Institute of Technology, Cambridge, MA.

Davidson, J., & diGregorio, S. (2011a). Qualitative research, technology, and global change. In N. Denzin & M. Giardina (Eds.), *Qualitative inquiry and the global crisis* (pp. 79-96). Walnut Creek, CA: Left Coast Press.

Davidson, J., & diGregorio, S. (2011b). Qualitative research and technology: In the midst of a revolution. In N. Denzin & Y. Lincoln (Eds.), *The SAGE Handbook of Qualitative Research* (4th ed.) (pp. 627-644). Thousand Oaks, CA: Sage Publications.

Davidson, J., Harris, A., Thompson, S., Tucker, L., & Ford, M. (2012, May). Teen talk about sexting: What it reveals about gender practices. In J. Davidson and L. A. Scheidt (Chairs), *Gender practices, technology, and adolescence: New perspectives from qualitative research.* Panel conducted at the Eighth Annual International Congress on Qualitative Inquiry, University of Illinois, Champaign, IL.

Davidson, J., & Koppenhaver, D. (1993). *Adolescent literacy: What works and why* (2nd ed.). New York: Garland Press.

Davidson, J., & Olson, M. (2003). School leadership in networked schools: Deciphering the impact of large technical systems on education. *International Journal of Leadership in Education, 6*(3), 261-281.

Davidson, J., Thompson, S., & Harris, A. (2014). Art as a tool to read social science data: Case study—teen sexting meets Jane Austen, Kara Walker, and Ryan Trecartin. *International Review of Qualitative Inquiry, 7*(2), 184-201.

diGregorio, S., & Davidson, J. (2008). *Qualitative research design for software users.* London: Open University Press/McGraw Hill.

Erickson, E. (1953/1963). *Childhood and society* [Kindle version]. Retrieved from Amazon.com.

Farman, J. (Ed.). (2014). *The mobile story: Narrative practices with locative technologies.* New York: Routledge.

Ford, M., Tucker, L., Thompson, S., Davidson, J., & Harris, A. (2012*). Sexting, youth, and society: An annotated bibliography.* Center for Women and Work Working Paper Series, Paper #12-01. Retrieved from http://www.uml.edu/research/centers/cww.

Foucault, M. (1995). *Discipline and punish* (2nd ed.). (A. Sheridan, Trans.). New York: Random House. (Original work published 1975

Gender. (n.d.). In *Wikipedia.* Retrieved May 20, 2014 from http://en.wikipedia.org/wiki/Gender

Griffin, S. (2001). *The book of the courtesans: A catalogue of their virtues.* New York: Broadway Books.

Griffin, S. (2011). *What her body thought: A journey into the shadows* [Kindle version]. Retrieved from Amazon.com

Harris, A., Davidson, J., Letourneau, C., Paternite, C., & Miofsky, K. (2013). *Building a prevention framework to address teen "sexting" behaviors.* Final report for Grant No. 2010-MC-CX-0001, awarded by the Office of Juvenile Justice and Delinquency Prevention Office of Justice Programs, U.S. Department of Justice. Available at: https://www.ncjrs.gov/pdffiles1/ojjdp/grants/244001.pdf

Hall, J., & Baym, N. (2011). Calling and texting (too much): Mobile maintenance expectations, (over)dependence, entrapment, and friendship satisfaction. *New Media & Society, 14*(2), 316-331. doi: 10. 1177/1461444811415047

Hesse-Biber, S. (Ed.). (2012). *Handbook of feminist research: Theory and practice* (2nd ed.). Thousand Oaks, CA: Sage.

Holson, L. (2012, April 25). 'What were you thinking?' for couples, new source of online friction. *The New York Times.* Retrieved July 2, 2014 from http://www.nytimes.com/2012/04/26/fashion/for-couples-new-source-of-online-friction.

Hu, E. (Presenter). (2013, September 27). Phantom phone vibrations: So common they've changed our brains? [Radio broadcast]. In *All Tech Considered.* Washington, DC: National Public Radio.

Hua, L. L. (2012). Sexting and social media in today's adolescent: Peer norms, problems, and provider responsibility. *The Brown University Child and Adolescent Behavior Letter, 28*(4), 1, 6.

Ito, M. (2010). *Hanging out, messing around, and geeking out: Kids living and learning with new media.* Cambridge, MA: MIT Press.

Kelly, K. (2005, February). How technology evolves [Video file]. Retrieved from https://www.ted.com/ talks/kevin_kelly_on_how_technology_evolves

Kelly, K. (2007, December). The next 5,000 days of the web [Video file]. Retrieved from http://www.ted.com/talks/kevin_kelly_on_the_next_5_000_days_of_the_web

Kelly, K. (2009, November). Technology's epic story [Video file]. Retrieved from http://www.ted.com/ talks/kevin_kelly_tells_technology_s_epic_story

Landry, M., Gonzales, F., Wood, S., & Vyas, A. (2013). New media use and sexual behavior among Latino adolescents. *American Journal of Health Behavior*, 37(3), 422-430. http://dx.doi.org/10.5993/AJHB.37.3.15

Lange, P. (2014). *Kids on YouTube: Technical identities and digital literacies*. Walnut Creek: Left Coast Press.

Lenhart, A. (2009). *Teens and sexting: How and why minor teens are sending sexually suggestive nude or nearly nude images via text messaging*. Pew Internet & American Life Project, Washington, DC. Retrieved from http://www.pewinternet.org/2009/12/15/teens-and-sexting/

Lenhart, A., Ling, R., Campbell, S., & Purcell, K. (2010). *Teens and mobile phones*. Pew Internet & American Life Project. Retrieved from http://www.pewinternet.org/2010/04/20/teens-and-mobile-phones/

Lenhart, A., Madden, M., Smith, A., Purcell, K., Zickuhr, K., & Rainie, L. (2011). *Teens, kindness and cruelty on social network sites*. Washington, DC: Pew Research Center.

Madden, M., Lenhart, A., Duggan, M., Cortesi, S., & Gasser, U. (2013). *Teens and technology 2013*. Pew Internet & American Life Project. Retrieved from http://www.pewinternet.org/2013/03/ 13/teens-and-technology-2013/

Marwick, A., Murgia-Diaz, D., & Palfrey, J. (2010). *Youth, privacy and reputation (literature review)*. Berkman Center Research Publication No. 2010-5. Abstract retrieved from http://ssrn.com/ abstract=1588163

McLean, K., & Mansfield, C. (2012). The co-construction of adolescent narrative identity: Narrative processing as a function of adolescent age, gender, and maternal scaffolding. *Developmental Psychology*, 48(2), 436-447.

Mitchell, K., Finkelhor, D., Jones, L., & Wolak, J. (2012). Prevalence and characteristics of youth sexting: A national study. *Pediatrics, 129*(1), 13-20. doi: 10.1542/peds.2011-1730

Mitchell, K., Wolak, J., & Finkelhor, D. (2007). Trends in youth reports of sexual solicitations, harassment and unwanted exposure to pornography on the Internet. *Journal of Adolescent Health, 40*(2), 116-126.

National Campaign to Prevent Teen and Unplanned Pregnancy. (2008). *Sex and tech: Results from a survey of teens and young adults*. Retrieved from http://thenationalcampaign.org/resource/sex-and-tech

Palfrey, J. (2008). *Enhancing child safety & online technologies: Final report of the Internet safety technical task force to the multi-state working group on social networking of state Attorneys General of the United States*. Berkman Center for Internet & Society at Harvard University. Retrieved from http://www.cap-press.com/pdf/1997.pdf

Parker, T., Blackburn, K., Perry, M., & Hawks, J. (2013). Sexting as an intervention: Relationship satisfaction and motivation considerations. *The American Journal of Family Therapy, 41*, 1-12. doi: 10.1080/01926187.2011.635134

Pasztory, E. (2005). *Thinking with things: Toward a new vision of art.* Austin, TX: University of Texas Press.

Perry, D., & Pauletti, R. (2011). Gender and adolescent development. *Journal of Research on Adolescence, 21*(1), 61-74.

Prensky, M. (2001). Digital natives, digital immigrants. *On the Horizon, 9*(5), 1-6. doi: 10.1108/ 10748120110424816

Rainey, D. (2008). Protecting your son from aggressive girls. Retrieved June 20, 2014, from http://www. familylife.com/articles/topics/parenting/challenges/sexual-purity/protecting-your-son-from-aggressive-girls#.U7F82rEmYtU

Ringrose, J., Gill, R., Livingstone, S., & Harvey, L. (2012). *A qualitative study of children, young people and 'sexting': A report prepared by the National Society for the Prevention of Cruelty to Children.* London: NSPCC.

Ringrose, J., Gill, R., Livingstone, S., & Harvey, L. (2013). Teen girls, sexual double standards and 'sexting': Gendered value in digital image exchange. *Feminist Theory, 14*(3), 305-323.

Root, A. K., & Denham, S. A. (2010). The role of gender in the socialization of emotion: Key concepts and critical issues. *New Directions for Child and Adolescent Development, 2010*, 1-9. doi: 10.1002/cd.265

Sexting. (n.d.). In *Wikipedia.* Retrieved May 20, 2014 from http://en.wikipedia.org/wiki/Sexting

Sexuality. (n.d.). In *Wikipedia.* Retrieved May 20, 2014, from http://en.wikipedia.org/wiki/Sexuality

Slut-shaming. (n.d.). In *Wikipedia.* Retrieved June 25, 2014 from http://en.wikipedia.org/siki/Slut-shaming

Strassberg, D. S., McKinnon, R. K., Sustaíta, M. A., & Rullo, J. (2013). Sexting by high school students: An exploratory and descriptive study. *Archives of Sexual Behavior, 42*(1), 15-21. doi: 10.1007/s10508-012-9969-8

Tanenbaum, L. (1999). *Slut! Growing up female with a bad reputation.* New York: Seven Stories Press.

Temple, J. R., Paul, J. A, Van den Berg, P., Le, V. D., McElhany, A., & Temple, B. W. (2012). Teen sexting and its association with sexual behaviors. *Archives of Pediatrics & Adolescent Medicine, 166*(9), 828-833. doi: 10.1001/archpediatrics.2012.835

Tolman, D. (2002). *Dilemmas of desire: Teenage girls talk about sexuality.* Cambridge, MA: Harvard University Press.

U.S. Department of State. (2008). Human trafficking defined. Retrieved from www.state.gov/j/tip/rls/ tiprpt/2008/105487.htm

Watkins, S. C. (2009). *The young and the digital: What the migration to social-network sites, games, and anytime, anywhere media means for our future.* Boston, MA: Beacon Press.

Weintrub, J. (2011, March 31). Always delete your sent box: Celebrities who've been caught sexting. In *HipHopWired*. Retrieved from http://hiphopwired.com/2011/03/31/always-delete-your-sent-box-celebrities-whove-been-caught-sexting-30097/

Weisskirch, R., & Delevi, R. (2012). Its ovr b/n u n me: Technology use, attachment styles, and gender roles in relationship dissolution. *Cyberpsychology, Behavior, and Social Networking, 15*(9), 486-490. doi: 10.1089/cyber.2012.0169

Wolak, J., Finkelhor, D., & Mitchell, K. J. (2012). How often are teens arrested for sexting? Data from a national sample of police cases. *Pediatrics, 129*(1), 4-12. doi: 10.1542/peds.2011-2242a2

INDEX

CPSIA information can be obtained at www.ICGtesting.com
Printed in the USA
BVOW02s0450130215

387429BV00002B/7/P